Military
Aircraft
of the 1970s

Gerry Manning

MIDLAND
An imprint of
Ian Allan Publishing

Military Aircraft of the 1970s
© 2007 Gerry Manning

ISBN (10) 1 85780 263 2
ISBN (13) 978 1 85780 263 4

Published by Midland Publishing
4 Watling Drive, Hinckley, LE10 3EY, England
Tel: 01455 254 490   Fax: 01455 254 495
E-mail: midlandbooks@compuserve.com

Midland Publishing is an imprint of
Ian Allan Publishing Ltd

Worldwide distribution (except North America):
Midland Counties Publications
4 Watling Drive, Hinckley, LE10 3EY, England
Telephone: 01455 254 450   Fax: 01455 233 737
E-mail: midlandbooks@compuserve.com
www.midlandcountiessuperstore.com

North American trade distribution:
Specialty Press Publishers & Wholesalers Inc.
39966 Grand Avenue, North Branch, MN 55056
Tel: 651 277 1400   Fax: 651 277 1203
Toll free telephone: 800 895 4585
www.specialtypress.com

Design concept
© 2007 Midland Publishing
Layout by Russell Strong

Printed in England
by Ian Allan Printing Ltd
Riverdene Business Park, Molesey Road,
Hersham, Surrey, KT12 4RG

Visit the Ian Allan Publishing website at:
www.ianallanpublishing.com

Introduction

This book is a follow-on to my *Military Aircraft of the 1960s* published in 2006.
The aim is to show the variants and types of military aircraft to be found during
the decade of the 1970s.

The world situation was one of the 'Cold War' raging yet despite this, for
much of the time, the West's aircraft could still be found in full colour markings
and almost every squadron showed a unit livery to indicate their ownership of
the aircraft. It was still possible to find a wide variety of types in service, from a
Meteor to a Tomcat, and from a Beverley to a Galaxy.

As with the 1960s book it was noticeable that many of the locations featured
in this work are no longer active airfields.

It is not possible in just over 300 pictures to show a whole decade of military
aviation so I have tried to show a variety of types and especially the squadrons
and air forces operating these.

Acknowledgements

It is always good to dip into other people's slide collections and I am indebted
to Phil Butler for the use of some of his pictures. Photographs without a credit
are my own.

Gerry Manning
Liverpool

Title page photograph:
Pictured landing at RAF Valley, in August 1976,
is a pair of based-No.4 FTS Hawker Hunters.
Nearest to the camera is single-seat F.6 XG209
coded 69 and the other, two-seat T.7 WV372
coded 85. The role of the unit was advanced flying
training.

The last all-British, single-seat interceptor fighter built for the Royal Air Force, the English Electric Lightning entered service with 74 Squadron in 1960. By the start of the 1970s, the early marks had been retired or re-tasked with training roles. Pictured at RNAS Yeovilton in July 1972 is **Lightning F.1A** XM177 of RAF Wattisham Target Facilities Flight. The unit supplied flying targets for radar intercepts by the front-line squadrons at the base. It was formed in March 1966 and disbanded at the end of 1973 as an economy measure. This was to save the cost of operating early F.1 and F.1A Lightnings whilst the operational units now flew F.3 and F.6 variants.

Pictured at RAF Binbrook in July 1975 is **Lightning F.1A** XM181/8415M. This airframe, once operated by the station TFF, is being used to test camouflage schemes for the front-line fleet. It is in an overall green scheme of the type adopted by the two West German-based units.

During the decade most Lightnings went from the glorious polished metal and full colour squadron markings to camouflage. Pictured at its RAF Binbrook base in May 1972 is **Lightning F.6** XR772 'E' of 5 Squadron, still in the 'real' markings of a fighter aircraft. The unit formed with the Lightning in October 1965 and stayed at Binbrook until the type's final withdrawal.

Pictured at its RAF Binbrook base in July 1974 is **Lightning F.6** XS925 'L' of 5 Squadron.

The camouflage scheme adopted for the UK-based units was a grey-green mix, as illustrated by this pair of RAF Binbrook-based 5 Squadron aircraft. **Lightning F.3** XP751 carries no unit markings but XP694 is coded 'R'. They are pictured at RAF Leuchars in September 1978.

11 Squadron reformed at RAF Leuchars in April 1967 with the Lightning. They moved in 1972 to RAF Binbrook, where they remained until the end of the Lightning's service in April 1988 and had the distinction of being the last operational unit with the type. Pictured in May 1972 at RAF Binbrook is **Lightning F.6** XR769 'J' of 11 Squadron. This aircraft is fitted with the long-range over-wing ferry tanks.

Lightning F.6 XR757 'D' of 11 Squadron is pictured at its RAF Binbrook base in July 1975.

Camouflage caught up with the unit, as it did with all squadrons. **Lightning F.3** XP741 'N' of 11 Squadron is pictured at its RAF Binbrook base in September 1977.

Seen landing at RAF Binbrook in August 1978 is **Lightning F.6** XR727 'F' of based 11 Squadron.

23 Squadron converted to Lightnings in August 1964 and spent its entire period on the type based at RAF Leuchars, before disbanding in October 1975. Pictured a month prior to this, at base, is **Lightning F.6** XR753 'A' of 23 Squadron. It has a white spine as a non-standard marking to the rest of the squadron.

Opposite page:

Pictured in the blast bays of RAF Leuchars, in September 1975, is **Lightning F.6** XS899 'E' of based-23 Squadron.

Lightning F.6 XS899 'E' of 23 Squadron is pictured leading two others back to its dispersal at RAF Leuchars in September 1975.

All the squadrons had two-seat trainers allocated for continuity training and standards ratings. **Lightning T.5** XS419 'T' of 23 Squadron is pictured at its RAF Leuchars base in September 1975.

56 Squadron *'The Firebirds'* had some of the most spectacular markings that the Lightning ever flew in. By the 1970s they had been toned down a degree. Pictured at Lakenheath in August 1975 is **Lightning F.6** XS897 'S' of 56 Squadron. The unit had become the second to convert to the type at the end of 1960; they relinquished the type for Phantoms in June 1976.

92 Squadron was one of two, with 19, to fly the F.2 variant of the Lightning. By the start of the 1970s these had been updated to F.2A standard, a version many thought to be the finest to fly. The unit spent the bulk of its life with RAF Germany. Pictured at RAF Valley in August 1976 on missile camp, is **Lightning F.2A** XN727 'W' of 92 Squadron. Despite the matt green upper surface paint it still has prominent its 'Cobra' tail markings.

Pictured landing at RAF Valley in August 1970 is **Lightning F.2A** XN782 'H' of 92 Squadron.

In August 1976, against a clear blue sky, **Lightning F.2A** XN726 'N' of 92 Squadron lands at RAF Valley.

92 Squadron's two-seat trainer, **Lightning T.4** XM994 'T' is pictured about to land at RAF Valley in August 1976 following a sortie to the local missile range. It is of note that the two-seater variant for the F.2A was the T.4 whilst the version for the F.3 and F.6 was the T.5.

92 Squadron disbanded with Lightnings at the end of March 1977, reforming the following day with Phantoms. It was sad to see their aircraft ending their days as target decoys. **Lightning F.2A** XN793 is pictured at RAF Wildenrath, West Germany in June 1978.

Formed in June 1963, No. 226 OCU (Operational Conversion Unit) was tasked with the training of Lightning pilots to type. The unit was a re-naming of the Central Fighter Establishment's Lightning Conversion Squadron. Pictured at RAF Chivenor in August 1970 is **Lightning F.3** XR716 '716' of 226 OCU/145 Squadron shadow.

During its lifespan 226 OCU had a number of 'shadow' units. This squadron number would be used by the instructors in time of war as an operational unit. Pictured at Upper Heyford in June 1971 is **Lightning F.1A** XM182 in the markings of 65 Squadron. This unit operated the F.1, F.1A and T.4 aircraft of the OCU.

Operating the F.3 and T.5s of 226 OCU was 2T Squadron. Its aircraft carried a blue nose flash and a stylised fin marking. Pictured at RAF Leuchars in September 1974 is **Lightning F.3** XP696. This aircraft has a white spine and was the solo aerobatic display aircraft for that year.

Pictured at RAF Binbrook in July 1974 is **Lightning F.3** XR716 of 2T/226 OCU. The RAF Coltishall-based unit disbanded in September of that year.

Pictured at RAF Coltishall in September 1971 is **Lightning T.5** XS450. Although devoid of markings it is operated by 226 OCU.

RAF Binbrook-based, the Lightning Training Flight grew from 'C' Flight of 11 Squadron. This unit had taken on the mantle of training new pilots following the disbandment of 226 OCU. It stood up in its new identity in October 1975. Pictured at base in August 1978 is **Lightning F.3** XP749 'A' of the LTF. The unit disbanded following completion of the last pilot's training in August 1987.

First flown in 1951, the Hawker Hunter had a long service life in the RAF and with many air forces worldwide. Pictured at Greenham Common in July 1976 is **Hunter FGA.9** XJ686 '41' of RAF Wittering-based 58 Squadron. This unit had a short life as a Hunter unit, being formed in August 1973 and disbanded in June 1976. Its role was to provide the RAF with a pool of pilots versed in the art of ground attack.

The Hunter, following its front-line duties, served as a training aircraft for the RAF. One of these roles was how to 'fight' an aircraft as a weapon of war following on from learning how to fly it. Pictured at RAF Binbrook in July 1975 is **Hunter F.6** XJ639 '31' of the TWU (Tactical Weapons Unit), shadow unit 234 Squadron. The TWU had been formed from 229 OCU in 1974 when it moved from RAF Chivenor to RAF Brawdy.

The role of No.4 FTS (Flying Training School) was to teach trainee pilots advanced flying instruction up to 'wings' standard. Their main equipment was the Folland Gnat and then, from 1976, the BAe Hawk. Hunters were operational with the prime task of training foreign pilots but RAF trainees who were too tall for the tiny Gnat's cockpit would also fly the Hunter. Pictured in August 1975 at its RAF Valley base is **Hunter F.6** XF509 '73' of No.4 FTS.

Pictured on approach to its RAF Valley base in August 1976 is **Hunter T.7** XL591 '82' of No.4 FTS. This variant was the two-seat, side-by-side trainer for the type. It is in the then Training Command colour scheme of red and white.

Hawker Hunters were operated on behalf of the Royal Navy by Airwork as the FRU (Fleet Requirements Unit). In October 1972 they moved from Hurn to RNAS Yeovilton and became first the FRADTU, and then the still current FRADU (Fleet Requirements and Aircraft Director Unit). The dropped 'T' stood for training. The role of the unit is to provide either radar or visual targets in air defence exercises for ships of the fleet. Pictured at Greenham Common in July 1973 is **Hunter GA.11** WV256 '732' of the FRADU.

As well as the single-seat Hunter, the FRADU operated the naval two-seater. Pictured at RAF Lossiemouth in September 1977 is **Hunter T.8** XE665 '878' of the FRADU. Both of the naval Hunters were equipped with arrester hooks but were for land-based operations only.

Pictured at RAF Coltishall in September 1971 is **Hunter T.7** XL616 of the ETPS (Empire Test Pilots School). This unit, based at Boscombe Down, is one of the premier schools of its type in the world, training both British and foreign students. One of the roles of the Hunter was to teach inverted spinning and recovery.

The Swiss Air Force was one of the largest users of the Hawker Hunter. They ordered the type in 1958 following evaluation of a number of fighters and continued flying them until 1994. The type served as the mount for the *Patrouille Suisse* national aerobatic team. One of the team, **Hunter F.58** J-4026, is pictured at Greenham Common in June 1979.

The Chilean Air Force was another of the export successes for the Hunter. They first operated the type in 1967 and over the years added to their fleet. Pictured at Chester in June 1971, prior to delivery, is **Hunter FGA.71** J-728. The Hunter was operated until 1995.

The SEPECAT Jaguar is a joint British and French low-level, single-seat attack aircraft. The first British aircraft flew in October 1969 from Warton, in the hands of veteran test pilot Jimmy Dell. This prototype **Jaguar SO.6 XW560** is pictured at a wet Boscombe Down in March 1971.

Pictured at RAF Wildenrath, West Germany in June 1978 is **Jaguar GR.1** XZ103 'I' of No. II (AC) Army Co-operation Squadron. With a history dating back to 1912 the unit always use Roman numerals rather than No 2. The RAF Laarbruch-based unit specialised in tactical reconnaissance.

Conversion training for the Jaguar was the task of 226 OCU. It stood up, as this, in October 1974 from the JCT (Jaguar Conversion Team). Pictured at RAF Binbrook in August 1978 is **Jaguar GR.1** XX758 '18' of 226 OCU.

Pictured at RAF Valley in August 1975 is **Jaguar T.2** XX142 'G' of 226 OCU. The T.2 was the two-seat trainer for the type.

The other nation in the Jaguar design, France, designated its aircraft as either Jaguar A for single-seat or Jaguar E for two-seat. During the operational lifespan of the type the French aircraft were not updated to as high a standard of specification as the RAF ones. Pictured in store at Châteaudun in June 1977 is **Jaguar E** E38.

Although no longer in service the Lockheed SR-71 set performance figures that have not been bettered by any announced aircraft. Pictured at Farnborough in September 1974 is **SR-71A** 64-17972 operated by the 9th SRW (Strategic Reconnaissance Wing) at Beale AFB in California. This aircraft had just broken the speed record for New York to London with a flight time of 1 hour 54 minutes. It later flew home setting a record for London to Los Angeles of 3 hours 47 minutes. This airframe is now on display at Dulles Airport, Washington DC.

Throughout the decade the McDonnell F-4 Phantom II was the most important and widely used Western warplane. Of the twelve nations that operated it ten still do to this day, albeit in some cases in limited or second-line duties. The first Phantom flew in May 1958 and was designed as an all-weather fleet defence interceptor for the US Navy. Pictured at Harlingen, Texas in October 1979 is **F-4J Phantom** 155748 205/AD of VF-171 *Aces*. Based at NAS Oceana, Virginia, it was the F-4 Fleet Replacement Squadron for the USN's Atlantic Fleet, its task being to train pilots on the type.

The US Marine Corps was an important user of the F-4, starting operations in June 1962. Over twenty-five squadrons flew the type, with the last operations in 1991. Pictured on the deck of USS *Nimitz* (CVN-68) in September 1975 is **F-4J Phantom** 153893 135/AJ of VMFA-333 *Shamrocks*. This unit scored the only USMC air-to-air kill in the Vietnam War when an F-4J shot down a MiG-21.

So good was the Phantom that the USAF bought it. This meant a lot of pride-swallowing to find a Navy aeroplane better than anything they had. Eventually the USAF became the largest operator of the type. The first variant in service was the F-4C, this was a basic USN F-4B with a list of USAF modifications that included ground attack capability, a set of dual controls in the back seat and even lower pressure tyres. Pictured on the ramp at Luke AFB, Arizona in October 1979 is **F-4C Phantom** 63-7428 of the 311th TFTS, part of the 58th Tactical Fighter Training Wing. Its role was advanced pilot training on the type.

Following the F-4C came the F-4D. This was the first USAF purpose-designed variant; it began service life in March 1966. Pictured at RAF Valley in August 1975 is **F-4D Phantom** 65-0667 of the 81st TFW (Tactical Fighter Wing) based at Woodbridge, Suffolk.

First flown in May 1964, the RF-4C was the dedicated reconnaissance variant with a re-designed nose to house the cameras. Pictured at RAF Wildenrath in June 1978 is **RF-4C Phantom** 68-0567 of the 17th TRS, part of the 26th TRW (Tactical Reconnaissance Wing) based at Zweibrücken, West Germany.

RF-4C Phantom 64-1070 of the 30th TRS, part of the 10th TRW, is pictured overflying RAF Coltishall in August 1975. The unit was based at Alconbury.

Pictured at Edwards AFB in October 1979 is **YF-4E Phantom** 65-0713 operated by the based AFFTC (Air Force Flight Test Centre). The airframe was the third trials aircraft for the gun-equipped F-4E. It had been felt at one time that missiles would be the future and the gun on a fighter was outdated. Operations in Vietnam proved this to be false and so the gun returned as a standard fitting.

Pictured at Upper Heyford in July 1976 is **F-4E Phantom** 74-1041 of the 32nd TFS (Tactical Fighter Squadron) based at Soesterberg, Holland. This variant was the production aircraft fitted with the internal cannon.

West Germany became a major user of the F-4, operating first reconnaissance and then fighter-bomber variants. Pictured at RAF Binbrook in July 1975 is **RF-4E Phantom** 35+81 of AKG (Aufklärungsgeschwader) 51 *Immelmann*, a Bremgarten-based photo reconnaissance unit.

The F-4F was a specially designed variant for the Luftwaffe. In basic terms it was a lightweight and simplified F-4E with a high content of West German-manufactured components. These were shipped to St Louis for final assembly. Pictured at RAF Binbrook in September 1977 is **F-4F Phantom** 37+86 of JG (Jagdgeschwader) 71 *Richthofen*, a Wittmundhafen-based fighter unit.

Replacing both F-104 Starfighters and F-86 Sabres, the F-4 joined the Spanish Air Force (Ejercito del Aire) in March 1971. Pictured landing at Greenham Common in June 1979 is **F-4C Phantom** C.12-40 of Torrejon-based Ala 12 (12 Wing). These aircraft were all secondhand USAF machines.

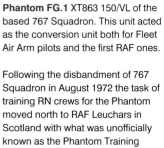

The first export customer for the F-4 was the Royal Navy. This variant was to be powered by a pair of Rolls-Royce Spey turbofans. Pictured at a wet RNAS Yeovilton in July 1972 is **Phantom FG.1** XT863 150/VL of the based 767 Squadron. This unit acted as the conversion unit both for Fleet Air Arm pilots and the first RAF ones.

Following the disbandment of 767 Squadron in August 1972 the task of training RN crews for the Phantom moved north to RAF Leuchars in Scotland with what was unofficially known as the Phantom Training Flight. Pictured at base in September 1972 is **Phantom FG.1** XV569 of the PTF with the short-lived 'LU' tail code. It was normal FAA policy to have two-letter codes indicating the aircraft's base, even though in this case the base was an RAF airfield.

The PTF soon took an official identity as the PPOCU (Phantom Post-Operational Conversion Unit). It adopted single-letter codes lacking the usual naval side numbers. Pictured at its RAF Leuchars base in September 1977 is **Phantom FG.1** XT866 'W' of the PPOCU. The unit disbanded in May of the following year.

The sole front-line operational squadron in the Fleet Air Arm operating the Phantom was 892. They formed in March 1969 at RNAS Yeovilton and moved to RAF Leuchars in July 1972 and used this station as its shore-base until they were disbanded following their aircraft carrier HMS *Ark Royal* being paid off in December 1978. Pictured taking off from base in September 1976 is **Phantom FG.1** XV587 010/R of 892 Squadron. It carries on the side of the fuselage the Royal Navy's flag: the White Ensign. Either side of it are the dates 876 and 1976. This was a dig at the American military, who were celebrating the nation's bi-centennial and had the US flag with 1776 and 1976 on many aircraft. It was the Senior Service showing who had the real history.

Pictured in September 1975 flying past at their RAF Leuchars shore base are **Phantom FG.1s** XV867 014/R and XT863 001/R of 892 Squadron.

With everything down, **Phantom FG.1** XT863 001/R of 892 Squadron flies low over RNAS Lee-on-Solent in July 1974.

Reformed in September 1969, 43 Squadron operated Phantoms surplus to FAA requirements. They were an air defence unit whilst the bulk of RAF operators were in the strike/attack role. **Phantom FG.1 XV578 'O'** is pictured landing at the unit's RAF Leuchars base in September 1974.

Taxying out to rehearse a display is **Phantom FG.1** XT873 'S' of 43 Squadron at its RAF Leuchars base in September 1976.

Pictured at its RAF Leuchars base in September 1974 is **Phantom FG.1** XV579 'R' of 43 Squadron. Note that it has its wings folded as it sits at its dispersal point.

October 1974 saw the formation, as a Phantom unit, of 111 Squadron at RAF Coningsby. November the following year saw a move to RAF Leuchars to be a second air defence unit at the base. **Phantom FGR.2** XT892 'K' of 111 Squadron is at its base in September 1976.

Flying the Phantom for just a few years was RAF Coningsby-based 41 Squadron. They reformed with the type in April 1972 and then in March 1977 converted to fly Jaguars. Their role remained the same, that of photographic reconnaissance. Pictured at RAF Leuchars in September 1974 is **Phantom FGR.2** XV418 of 41 Squadron.

Another short-lived Phantom squadron was 54. They equipped at RAF Coningsby in September 1969 in a strike/attack role and converted to Jaguars in April 1974. Pictured at RAF Leuchars in September 1972 is **Phantom FGR.2** XV434 'G' of 54 Squadron.

RAF Bruggen-based 31 Squadron officially reformed with the Phantom in October 1971 in the strike/attack role having previously flown Canberras. Pictured at RAF Coningsby in August 1976 is **Phantom FGR.2** XV494 in the squadron's colours. The unit had finished its conversion to the Jaguar the previous month.

Officially reformed on the Phantom in January 1975, 29 Squadron was tasked with air defence. Pictured at its RAF Coningsby base in August 1976 is **Phantom FGR.2** XV423 'P' of 29 Squadron. The unit flew the Phantom until 1987 when they started Tornado F.3 operations.

One of two West German-based air defence units, 19 Squadron converted to Phantoms from Lightnings at the end of 1976. Pictured at RAF Wildenrath, the unit's base, in June 1978 is **Phantom FGR.2** XT901 'B' of 19 Squadron. The unit disbanded in January 1992.

To convert trainee Phantom pilots to type was the role of 228 OCU. They were officially formed in August 1968 and in July 1970 adopted the shadow identity of 64 Squadron. Pictured departing the unit's RAF Coningsby base in August 1976 are **Phantom FGR.2s** XV393 and XV394 of 228 OCU/64 Squadron.

To commemorate the 60th anniversary of the 1919 first non-stop flight across the Atlantic Ocean, in a Vickers Vimy, by Alcock and Brown, Squadron Leader Tony Alcock and Flight Lieutenant Norman Brown, one being a direct descendant of the original crew, recreated the flight albeit at a much faster pace in a Phantom. Pictured at RAF Abingdon in September 1979 is **Phantom FGR.2** XV424 in its special livery for the event.

The first of the 'Century Series' of fighters was the North American F-100 Super Sabre. As well as USAF use it served with France, Denmark and Turkey in NATO. The French operated one hundred of the type from 1958 to the mid-1970s when the survivors were mostly flown to Sculthorpe under the terms of the Military Aid Program that had funded their supply. Pictured at this location in May 1976 is **F-100D Super Sabre** 42165 11-ML of EC 2/11 (Escadre de Chasse) *Vosges* of the French Air Force.

The two-seat variant of the Super Sabre was designated F-100F. Pictured at Bentwaters in May 1970 is **F-100F Super Sabre** GT-018 of the Royal Danish Air Force. It is in its original bare metal finish and is operated by Skrydstrup-based Eskadrille 727.

During the decade the Danes toned down the size of the markings and painted the aircraft an overall green. Pictured at RAF Leuchars in September 1976 is **TF-100F Super Sabre** GT-874. The 'TF' designation was for a number of F-100Fs delivered to Denmark from USAF stocks prior to being brought up to Danish standard.

The second of the 'Century Series' was the McDonnell F-101 Voodoo. It was designed as a long-range fighter for SAC (Strategic Air Command) and went on to serve in most USAF commands as well as the air forces of Canada and the Nationalist Chinese. Pictured at Edwards AFB in October 1979, is **F-101B Voodoo** 58-0329 of the 123rd FIS (Fighter Interceptor Squadron) Oregon ANG. This Portland-based unit flew the type from 1971 to 1982.

The next in the series was the Convair F-102. This interceptor was a complete weapons system. Pictured at RAF Leuchars in September 1972 is **F-102A Delta Dagger** 56-1418 of Keflavik, Iceland-based 57th FIS *The Black Knights*.

Together with the Phantom the Lockheed Starfighter was the most widely used NATO warplane during the decade. Its design in the 1950s with a pencil-slim fuselage and thin sharp wings was years ahead of its rivals in style, but not always in performance. Pictured at Luke AFB. Arizona in October 1979, is **F-104G Starfighter** 67-14890 of the based 58th TTW. Although in American markings this unit was operated by the Luftwaffe to train its pilots making full use of the good weather conditions of the state.

When a number of NATO nations bought the F-104, in what was known as 'the sale of the century', the bulk of the production was not from the Lockheed factory. In Canada Canadair produced the CF-104 for the RCAF (later CAF). Pictured at Upper Heyford in June 1971 is **CF-104G Starfighter** 104865. It is fitted with a Vicon reconnaissance pod on the underside of the fuselage. This could house up to four 70mm Vinten cameras. This aircraft is in the early bare metal silver finish.

By the middle of the decade an overall dark green paint scheme had covered the CAF Starfighters. Pictured at Upper Heyford in July 1976 is two-seat **CF-104D Starfighter** 104653 of 439 Squadron, then based at Baden-Sollingen in West Germany.

The NATO 'Tiger Meet' can always be relied upon to produce some wonderful non-standard liveries. Pictured at Upper Heyford in July 1976 is **CF-104G Starfighter** 104756 of 439 Squadron. The Canadians had painted the whole aircraft in tiger colours. The origins of the meet go back to when three squadrons of the RAF, USAF and French Air Force, who had a tiger as their unit badge, got together for an informal exchange. From this it has grown to be a full-blown NATO event.

Starfighters for the Dutch Air Force were licence-built by Fokker in Holland. Pictured at RAF Leuchars in September 1974 is **F-104G Starfighter** D-8311 of 323 Squadron. This Leeuwarden-based unit was tasked with all-weather interception and flew the type from 1964 to 1980.

Following a series of defence cuts in Canada, Norway purchased a number of Canadian-built Starfighters in the early part of the decade. **CF-104G Starfighter** 104755 is pictured at Upper Heyford in July 1976. This aircraft was operated by Bodo-based 331 Skv, who flew the type from 1963 to 1981.

Pictured at RAF Wildenrath in June 1978 is Belgian Air Force **F-104G Starfighter** FX-76 of Kleine Brogel-based 10 Wing. This nation's aircraft were assembled locally by SABCA. It is of note that this aircraft has the code letter 'A'. This is for a Tactical Weapons Meet being held at the base, Belgian aircraft are not usually coded.

Italy was the last nation to dispose of its Starfighters, keeping them in service, albeit much updated, until 2004. Like most nations in NATO the aircraft were locally assembled, in their case by Fiat. Pictured at Upper Heyford in June 1971 is **F-104S Starfighter** MM6728 53-14 of 21 Gruppo/53 Stormo based at Cameri. The F-104S was a local conversion of the F-104G in a collaboration between Aeritalia, Lockheed and the Italian Air Force. It had improved performance, weapons lift and electronics.

West Germany was the largest user of the Starfighter. 917 were operated, 766 for the Luftwaffe and 151 for the Marineflieger. It achieved notoriety due to its high loss rate and the deaths of the pilots. Over 250 airframes were destroyed; however this was a lower percentage than some other NATO air forces. Pictured at RAF Wildenrath in June 1978 is **F-104G Starfighter** 21+98 of JBG 33 based at Buchel. This aircraft is carrying the code letter 'E' for its participation in a NATO weapons meet at the base. Luftwaffe aircraft do not usually have codes.

Since West Germany had so many F-104s they were built in a number of locations. Initially Lockheed at Marietta, then Fiat in Turin, SABCA in Belgium, Fokker in Holland, and Messerschmitt in West Germany. Pictured at Lakenheath in August 1975 is Lockheed-built two-seat **TF-104G Starfighter** 27+34 of Buchel-based JBG 33.

Pictured at Greenham Common in June 1979 is Fiat-built **F-104G Starfighter** 21+18 of Eggebeck-based MFG-2 of the Marineflieger. This unit operated the Starfighter from 1965 to 1986.

The Republic Thunderchief was an all-weather strike fighter. In the early years of the Vietnam War it bore the brunt of operations over the north and lost 397 aircraft in the process. Pictured at Lakenheath in October 1976 is **F-105D Thunderchief** 61-0093 operated by the 121st TFS/113th TFW District of Columbia ANG.

District of Columbia ANG **F-105D Thunderchief** 61-0093 heads a line of the Andrews AFB-based unit on a squadron strength deployment to Lakenheath in October 1976.

Also at Lakenheath in October 1976 was a squadron of F-105s from the 149th TFS/192nd TFG Virginia ANG based at Richmond. Heading the line is **F-105D Thunderchief** 61-0164.

To train pilots on the big F-105 a two-seat variant was produced. This was the F-105F. Pictured at Lakenheath in October 1976, with both cockpits open, is **F-105F Thunderchief** 62-4414 operated by the 149th TFS/192nd TFG of the Virginia ANG.

The 'Wild Weasel' variant of the F-105 was a dedicated anti-radar and ground-to-air missile site attack aircraft. They were all two-seaters and used missiles designed to home in on the emissions from ground-based radar sets. Pictured at Edwards AFB in October 1979, is **F-105G Thunderchief** 63-8332 of the 35th TFW based at George AFB, California. Note that the unit's tail code reflects its role.

The elegant Convair F-106 was the last pure interceptor operated by the USAF. It flew in an era of full colour markings and operated from 1959 to 1988 in both Air Defence Command and the Air National Guard. Pictured at George AFB, California in October 1979 is **F-106A Delta Dart** 57-2495 of Castle AFB-based 84th FIS.

Pictured at Edwards AFB in October 1979 is **F-106A Delta Dart** 58-0782 of the 194th FIS California ANG. Home-based at Fresno, this aircraft has the state symbol of a bear on the fin. The unit flew the type from 1974 for ten years, when they were then replaced by F-4 Phantoms.

First flown in July 1959, the Northrop F-5 Freedom Fighter went against the current trend of large complex multi-role aircraft. It was a simple light-weight fighter that was supplied to air forces around the world. Many still operate it, having had the avionics updated. Pictured at RAF Binbrook in September 1977 is **Northrop NF-5A** K-3031 of Gilze-Rijen-based 316 Squadron, Royal Netherlands Air Force.

One of the roles that the USAF F-5s operated in was that of an 'aggressor' squadron to train operational fighter pilots in air combat manoeuvring against a dissimilar type of aircraft. The European unit, formed in April 1976, was based at Alconbury and the aircraft were in different colour schemes and camouflage patterns to reflect various operating environments. Pictured, at base, in October 1978 is **Northrop F-5E** 74-1559 of the 527th TFTAS (Tactical Fighter Training & Aggressor Squadron).

When the Chilean Air Force obtained fifteen single-seat F-5Es they also received three two-seat F-5Fs. These are currently operated by the 7th Fighter Squadron based in the north of the country at Cerro Moreno. Pictured at Edwards AFB in October 1976, prior to delivery, is **Northrop F-5F Tiger** J-815 (ex 75-0709). (Phil Butler)

Pictured at RAF Valley in August 1975 is two-seat **Northrop F-5B** 135 (ex 68-7135) of Rygge-based 336 Squadron Royal Norwegian Air Force. The type serves to this day.

Neutral non-aligned Sweden has long had a reputation for building very advanced warplanes for its own air force. First flying in October 1955 was the Saab 35 Draken (Dragon). As well as home use it was exported to Finland, Denmark and Austria. The aircraft had a Mach-2 performance from a single Rolls-Royce Avon engine licence-built by Volvo. Pictured at Lakenheath in August 1975 is two-seat **SK-35XD Draken** AT-154 of 729 Esk Royal Danish Air Force. This unit was based at Karup.

Sweden followed the Draken with the multi-role Saab 37 Viggen (Thunderbolt). This type was not exported and served with the Swedish Air Force until 2005 when they were withdrawn following defence cuts. Its roles included interceptor, attack, reconnaissance and electronic warfare. Pictured at Paris-Le Bourget in June 1977 is **SH-37 Viggen** 37909 '17' of Norrkoping-based F13 Wing.

One of the most successful French-built fighters was the Dassault Mirage III. The design first flew in November 1956 and the first fighter variant flew in October 1960. Pictured at Châteaudun in June 1977 is **Mirage 111C** No.44 10-ST of EC 1/10 *Valois* based at Creil.

The Mirage 5 was developed for Israel. It was a daylight-only ground-attack version of the Mirage III. The prototype first flew in May 1967. Before deliveries could begin the French government, under President de Gaulle, placed an arms embargo on Israel and they were never delivered. The aircraft were stored and then delivered to the French Air Force as the Mirage 5F. Pictured, whilst in store at Châteaudun, in June 1977 is **Mirage 5F** No.16.

France did sell the Mirage 5 to other countries, with at least a dozen operating the type from Abu Dhabi to Zaire. Pictured at Upper Heyford in July 1976 is **Mirage 5BA** BA-26 of Florennes-based 2 Smaldeel/2 Wing, Belgian Air Force.

Following on in the role of interceptor from the Mirage III came the Mirage F1. The prototype flew in December 1966, with the first French Air Force units equipping in 1974. The design also sold well in the export market with at least ten nations purchasing the type. Pictured at RAF Leuchars in September 1974 is **Mirage F1** No.24 30-FB of Reims-based ECTT3/30 *Lorraine*.

With France now unwilling to sell aircraft to the Israelis, they set about producing their own unlicensed copy of the Mirage 5 by using stolen plans; this was the Dagger. Following the experience with this, they produced the Kfir (Lion Cub) powered by a US-supplied General Electric J79 engine. Pictured at Paris-Le Bourget in June 1977 is **IAI Kfir C2** 4X-CFL/779 of the Israeli Air Force. The C2 variant was the first fully equipped version and had nose strakes and fixed canard foreplanes.

A carrier-based single-seat strike aircraft, the Dassault Etendard IV first flew in July 1958. A second production batch was built as a photographic reconnaissance version with a 'P' suffix in the designation. Pictured at RAF Chivenor in August 1970 is **Etendard IVP** No.106 of Landivisiau-based 16 Flotille of France's Aeronavale.

The Grumman Intruder first flew in April 1969. Its role was that of day or night, carrier-based, all-weather attack bomber with a crew of two in a side-by-side seating configuration. It has served both with the US Navy and the US Marine Corps. Pictured at Greenham Common in July 1976 is **A-6E Intruder** 154126 502/AE of VA-176 *Thunderbolts*. This Oceana-based unit was operating from USS *America* (CVA-66) at the time.

Pictured at Mildenhall in August 1978 is **A-6E Intruder** 160424 501/AB of VA-34 *Blue Blasters*. Oceana-based, the squadron equipped with the type in 1970. It was part of the USS *John F. Kennedy* (CVA-67) wing when pictured.

To add flight refuelling capacity to the fleet and to avoid the logistical problems of a new type on the ship's decks, old A-6A airframes were converted to flying tankers with the designation KA-6D. The first conversion flew in May 1966 and had a hose-reel unit fitted to the rear fuselage. Pictured on board USS *Nimitz* (CVA-68) in September 1975 is **KA-6D Intruder** 152913 523/AJ of VA-35 *Black Panthers*. It heads a line of the squadron and features full size and colour markings now sadly gone from US Navy aircraft.

Pictured at NAS Lemoore, California in October 1979 is **KA-6D Intruder** 151801 520/NK of VA-196 *Main Battery*. Shore-based at Whidbey Island, Washington they operated from USS *Coral Sea* (CV-43) when at sea.

The Grumman Prowler was the USN's standard carrier-based electronic warfare aircraft. The airframe was based upon the Intruder but extended to fit a second cockpit to take two extra members of crew who handled the various items of jamming equipment. Pictured on board USS Nimitz (CVA-68) in September 1975 is **EA-6B Prowler** 158542 612/AJ of VAQ-130 Zappers. This unit was the first to be equipped with the type and was shore-based at Whidbey Island, Washington.

Pictured at Greenham Common in June 1977, with both cockpits open, is **EA-6B Prowler** 158802 612/AB of VAQ-133 Wizards, then based aboard USS John F Kennedy (CVA-67). In 1973 they were the first unit to operate the EXCAP (Expanded Capability) variant of the type. They were disbanded in 1992.

The Vought Corsair II was developed as a single-seat, light-attack and ship-board aircraft for the US Navy. It first flew in September 1965 and was so successful in its role that the USAF bought it. It was a rare event for them to purchase a Navy aircraft. Pictured at NAS Lemoore, California in October 1979 is **A-7B Corsair II** 154520 '312' of VA-303 *Golden Hawks*. This based unit was a reserve squadron. The 'B' model had a more powerful engine than the underpowered 'A' variant.

The TF-30 engine of the early variants of the A-7 was replaced with the Allison TF-41 (which was a development of the Rolls-Royce Spey). The new version, designated A-7E, was regarded as the definitive variant. Pictured at NAS Lemoore, the West Coast base for the type, in October 1979 is **A-7E Corsair II** 157497 303/NK of VA-97 *Warhawks* then based upon USS *Coral Sea* (CV-43).

Pictured at NAS Lemoore, California in October 1979 is A-7E Corsair II 157536 400/NK of VA-27 *The Royals*. This aircraft has extra colour markings on the rudder as it is the personal aircraft of the unit's commanding officer, it was carrier-based upon USS *Coral Sea* (CV-43).

Another CO's aircraft at NAS Lemoore in October 1979 is **A-7E Corsair II** 158021 400/NH of VA-195 *The Dam Busters*. This unit, based aboard USS *America* (CVA-66), acquired its name during the Korean War following raids on North Korean dams in May 1951.

When one looks at the current lack of colour on USN aircraft one can only look back in wonder at the days of full colour markings when the squadron's CO and the carrier's CAG (Commander Air Group) had even more special colours added. Pictured at NAS Lemoore in October 1979 is **A-7E Corsair II** 157516 401/NE with 'CO' on the fin tip of VA-25 *Fist of the Fleet*. The unit was carrier-based upon USS *Ranger* (CVA-61).

The two-seat conversion trainer for the Corsair II was not flown until 1972 and entered service long after the single-seat front-line version. Pictured at NAS Lemoore in October 1979 is **TA-7C Corsair II** 156795 204/NJ of VA-122 *Flying Eagles*. This was a training squadron for the type and has the titles of carrier USS *Lexington* (CV-16). This ship was based at NAS Pensacola, Florida and used as the training carrier for pilot qualification on ships. It served in this role until the end of 1991 when USS *Forrestal* (CVA-59) took on this task.

The A-7 had been developed from the layout of the Vought Crusader. It was a single-seat, single-engine, carrier-based fighter and known in the US Navy as 'the last of the gunfighters'. By the 1970s those still in service were tasked with the role of photographic reconnaissance. Pictured on board USS *John F. Kennedy* (CVA-67) in October 1976 is **RF-8G Crusader** 144607 602/AB of VFP-63 *Eyes of the Fleet*. This squadron was the last dedicated PR unit, flying the last dedicated PR aircraft in US Navy service. VFP-63 flew the type for twenty-one years until 1982. The square camera ports can be seen on either side of the stars and bars national markings.

The last user of the F-8 was the French Navy who operated them from their carriers until 1999. Pictured at RNAS Yeovilton in July 1972 is **F-8E(FN) Crusader** No.40 of Landivisiau-based 12 Flotille.

One of the best light-attack aircraft of all time has been the Douglas Skyhawk. A carrier-based, single-seat, single-engined delta wing aircraft, it first flew in June 1954 and entered service with the US Navy in 1956. Over the years both airframe and powerplants have been upgraded and it can still be found in service today following extensive export sales. Seen at Greenham Common in June 1977 is **A-4G Skyhawk** N13-155051 '870' of VF805 Squadron Royal Australian Navy. This unit was shore-based at RANAS Nowra and at sea upon HMAS *Melbourne*. The air arm ceased fixed-wing operations in 1984 when their only carrier was retired.

Pictured at Edwards AFB in October 1979 is **A-4F Skyhawk** 155031 302/UH of VC-7. This aircraft is allocated to the squadrons Executive Office and has the 'XO' initials on the fin tip. The unit is a Fleet Composite Squadron based at NAS Miramar.

By the end of the decade the early signs of a tone-down in US Navy livery were starting. Pictured at NAS Lemoore in October 1979 is **TA-4F Skyhawk** 154334 04/NJ of based VA-127. This aircraft is the two-seat training version of the type.

Following a 1954 NATO request for a lightweight fighter and ground attack aircraft, the winner of the design competition was the Fiat G.91. It was operated by the Italian, Portuguese and West German air forces and even evaluated by the US Army. Pictured at Lakenheath in August 1975 is licence-built **Dornier G.91R.3** 32+82 of Oldenburg-based LKG -43 (Light Combat Wing).

The two-seat training variant of the G.91 was designated G.91T and was operated by both training and front-line units. Pictured at RAF Binbrook in September 1977 is an original Italian-built **Fiat G.91T-1** 34+33 operated by Luftwaffe unit LKG-43. This Oldenburg-based aircraft has lots of high-visibility Day-Glo on it.

The quest for a practical working VTOL (Vertical Take-Off and Landing) aircraft was a long one and produced many varied ideas. Most had two sets of engines, one for take-off and the other for horizontal flight. This was impractical as the aircraft had to carry the weight penalty of a set of engines that were only used during the take-off and landing phase of flight. With the Hawker P.1127 the problem was solved by having just one engine whose nozzles rotated from down for take-off to back for level flight. From this research prototype, via the Kestrel, came the Harrier. Pictured at RAF Valley in August 1973 is **Hawker Siddeley Harrier GR.1** XV741 'A' of 3 Squadron. This unit was part of the 2nd TAF (Tactical Air Force) based at RAF Laarbruch, West Germany.

Following the original GR.1 Harrier came the more capable GR.3. This variant had a longer nose to house its laser range finder and a radar warning receiver on the leading edge of the fin. Pictured at RAF Leuchars in September 1976 is **Harrier GR.3** XZ128 '15' of 1 Squadron. This RAF Wittering-based unit was the first squadron to operated the type and can claim to be the oldest military flying unit in the world, its history starting with a balloon unit in 1878.

The original core of Harrier pilots had to convert to type without the aid of a two-seat trainer, this following a year later. Pictured at RAF Valley in August 1973 is **Harrier T.2** XW926 'M' of Laarbruch-based 3 Squadron RAF.

For its role as a ground attack aircraft and 'tank buster' the Fairchild A-10 was designed around its central weapon, the GUA-8A Gatling gun. It won a competition for the production order over the Northrop A-9. Pictured at Paris-Le Bourget in June 1977 is **Fairchild A-10A** 75-0293 of the 355th TFW based at Davis-Monthan AFB, Arizona.

Entering service with the RAF in February 1956 the Gloster Javelin was a two-seat, all-weather, delta-wing fighter equipped with de Havilland Firestreak air-to-air missiles. By the 1970s just one aircraft was left flying. It was on charge to the Boscombe Down-based A&AEE (Aeroplane and Armament Experimental Establishment). **Javelin FAW.9** XH897 is pictured at RAF Coltishall in September 1971.

First flown in September 1952, the Dassault Mystère IVA served with the air forces of France, Israel and India. Pictured at Sculthorpe in May 1976 is **Mystère IVA** No.295 8-NA in the markings of weapons training unit ET 2/8 *Nice* based at Cazaux. It has the unit's badge of a black and white stork on the fin.

Following on in French service came the Dassault Super Mystère, this was a single-seat, supersonic interceptor and fighter-bomber. The prototype first flew in March 1955 and the type retired in September 1977. Pictured at Upper Heyford in June 1971 is **Super Mystère B2** No.88 12-YD of Cambrai-based EC 1/12 *Cambresis*. This unit is the French participant in the annual NATO Tiger Meet, note the badge on the fin.

Entering service with the RAF in 1944 the Gloster Meteor had a very long life in uniform. Pictured at RAF Woodvale in September 1971 is **Meteor F.8** WH453 operated by based No.5 CAACU (Civilian Anti-Aircraft Co-operation Unit). Its role was to provide aerial targets for gunners.

One of the brightest colour schemes for the Meteor was that of the drone version, this could operate without a pilot. Based at RAE Llanbedr, the majority of the aircraft were shot down during missile tests. Pictured at RAF Valley in August 1973 is **Meteor U.16** WA991 'F' of the RAE (Royal Aircraft Establishment).

One of the many 'one-offs' used by the A&AEE at Boscombe Down was **Meteor NF.13** WM367. This tropicalized version of the NF.11 night-fighter is pictured at base in March 1971.

The training version of the Meteor was the T.7. Pictured at RAF Coltishall in September 1971 is **Meteor T.7** WA669 '27' of the CFS (Central Flying School). This aircraft was operated for airshow work as one half of *The Vintage Pair*.

Operated as the other half of *The Vintage Pair* is **de Havilland Vampire T.11** XK624 '32' of the CFS. It is pictured at RAF Coltishall in September 1971. The side-by-side advanced trainer was developed from the single-seat fighter that entered RAF service in 1946.

The de Havilland Sea Vixen was a swept-wing, two-seat, all-weather interceptor for the Fleet Air Arm. Service entry was with 892 Squadron in July 1958 at RNAS Yeovilton. Pictured at Boscombe Down in March 1971 in a non-standard all-white colour scheme is **Sea Vixen FAW.1** XJ476 operated by the based A&AEE.

The next variant of the Sea Vixen was the FAW.2. It had forward extended booms to hold more fuel and was able to carry the Red Top air-to-air missile. Aircraft were both new-builds and conversions from FAW.1s. Pictured at Greenham Common in July 1973 is **Sea Vixen FAW.2** XJ572. Operated by the RNAY at Sydenham, Northern Ireland, it has the tail badge of the 'Red Hand of Ulster'. This airframe was one that had started life as an FAW.1 and had been converted at the de Havilland factory at Chester.

Pictured on board HMS *Eagle* in February 1970 is **Sea Vixen FAW.2** XJ584 '124/E' of 899 Squadron. When ashore this unit was based at RNAS Yeovilton. This airframe was also converted from an FAW.1 but at RNAY Sydenham, Belfast. (Phil Butler)

By the 1970s the North American Sabre was only in service with a few air forces or used as target drones. Pictured at Edwards AFB in October 1979, is **QF-86H Sabre** 53-1409 operated by the US Navy from its China Lake test site. The 'Q' designation represents a drone.

When the US Army wanted drones for its White Sands Missile Range in New Mexico, the Sabres they obtained were Canadian-built and ex-RCAF airframes. Pictured at Mojave, California in October 1979 is **Canadair Sabre 5** 23320/N74170. Re-designated as a QF-86E, this aircraft was shot down in August 1980.

Entering service during the decade, the McDonnell Douglas F-15 Eagle became the USAF's front-line fighter replacing the F-4 Phantom. Pictured at Luke AFB in October 1979 is **F-15A Eagle** 73-0087 of the based 405th TTW. This unit's task was training pilots on the type.

To facilitate the conversion of pilots to type the 405th TTW operated a number of two-seat Eagles. Pictured at its Luke AFB base in October 1979 is **F-15B Eagle** 76-0135.

Whilst the USAF had the F-15 the US Navy commenced operations with their premier fleet-defence fighter, the Grumman F-14 Tomcat. The two-seat aircraft proved itself in combat and was only retired in 2006, leaving just Iran to operate the type. Pictured at Paris-Le Bourget in May 1973 is **F-14A Tomcat** 158621 410/NJ of VF-124 *Gunfighters*. Based at NAS Miramar this unit was the West Coast Fleet Replenishment Squadron. Its role was the training of both front- and back-seat crew for the Tomcat.

For most of the decade the US Navy had very attractive full colour markings on their aircraft. Pictured at Greenham Common in July 1976 is **F-14A Tomcat** 159449 212/AE of VF-142 *Ghostriders*. Part of Carrier Air Wing CVW-6 aboard USS *America* (CVA-66), their shore base was NAS Oceana, Virginia.

Pictured on board USS *John F. Kennedy* (CVA-67) in October 1976 is **F-14A Tomcat** 159593 120/AB of VF-14 *Tophatters*. This unit converted to the type in 1974 and was East Coast-based at NAS Oceana.

Basic pilot training in the USAF has long been the provenance of the T-37. A side-by-side trainer, it entered service in 1957. Pictured at Williams AFB, Arizona in October 1979 is **Cessna T-37B** 67-14759 of the based 82nd FTW.

The T-37 has been exported to a number of nations. The air force of Portugal used the type as the platform for its *Asas de Portugal* aerobatic team. **Cessna T-37C** 2406 heads a line of the team at Greenham Common in June 1977.

The A-37 was a development of the T-37. Its role was a light-attack aircraft, for which it had eight hard-points under the wings, a more powerful engine and provision for in-flight refuelling. The US military used it in Vietnam and, later, with a number of ANG units. Pictured at Edwards AFB in October 1979 is **Cessna A-37B** 70-1307 operated by the based AFFTC (Air Force Flight Test Centre).

Entering service in 1961, and with no current replacement planned, the Northrop T-38 has provided the advanced training for several generations of America's fast jet pilots. Pictured at its Williams AFB base in October 1979 is **T-38A Talon** 64-13198 of the 82nd FTW.

The USAF *Thunderbirds* formation display team operated the T-38 in the latter part of the decade, having previously flown the F-4 Phantom. Pictured at Harlingen, Texas in October 1979 is **T-38A Talon** No.5 of the team. They are unusual in that the aircraft do not usually show their serial numbers.

Developed in Sweden as a side-by-side seating jet trainer, the Saab 105 has also been exported to Austria. Pictured flying at Greenham Common in June 1979 is **Saab 105OE** 428/H of the Austrian *Karo As* team based at Zeltweg.

One of the most widely used jet trainers is the Lockheed T-33. It was based upon the earlier P-80 and first flew in March 1948 with the designation TP-80C; this was changed to T-33A in May the following year. Over 6500 aircraft have been built. Pictured at a wet Upper Heyford in June 1971 is **T-33A Shooting Star** 1920 operated at BA1 Sintra by the Portuguese Air Force.

The Royal Netherlands Air Force was one of the many NATO air arms operating the T-33. Pictured at Upper Heyford in June 1971 is **T-33A Shooting Star** M-43. This aircraft had been supplied by Belgium, a country Holland had a joint training agreement with. It was returned to them the following year, with the Belgian serial FT-4, and written off in April 1977.

The first post-war generation of West German pilots did their advanced training on the T-33. Pictured at Greenham Common in July 1974 is **T-33A Shooting Star** 9500 of Furstenfeldbruck-based flying training unit WS-50.

With the large number of airframes available it was only natural that many T-33s would be used as testbeds for various trials. Pictured at Edwards AFB in October 1979 is **NT-33A Shooting Star** 51-4120. Note that the nose of this aircraft has been extended to house test instruments for the F-94 Starfire program. Following this it was used for variable-stability research to simulate the flying qualities of other aircraft types then under development. The 'N' prefix indicates a permanent conversion for test purposes.

French designed and built, the Fouga Magister was a widely used trainer and light-attack aircraft. It had two engines, albeit low power Turbomeca Marboré 11A turbojets of 880lb (400kg) static thrust. It was distinctive with its 'V'-shaped tail and the fact that it was not equipped with ejector seats. Pictured in August 1977 at its Baldonnel/Casement base is Irish Air Corps **CM.170 Magister** 215. The air arm operated six and they were able to carry light armaments.

Pictured landing at RAF Leuchars in September 1974 is **CM.170 Magister** MT-15 of the Belgian Air Force *Diables Rouges* (Red Devils) aerobatic team. The team have since disbanded but the air arm continues to operate small numbers of the type in various roles.

Throughout the decade all RAF pilot training was flown on the Jet Provost. This side-by-side basic trainer was designed to give *ab initio* courses to would-be pilots. Pictured at RAF Valley in August 1973 is **Jet Provost T.5** XW336 from the RAF College Cranwell's aerobatic team *The Poachers*. This variant was the first to be pressurised and had a redesigned canopy. It has long been a tradition of RAF Cranwell-based aircraft to have a light blue fuselage band; this aircraft has it in the form of a stripe up the fin.

Pictured at RAF Leuchars in September 1977 is **Jet Provost T.5B** XW306 'Y' of RAF Finningley-based No.6 FTS. The role of this training unit was to teach navigators their art.

Pictured lined up at RAF Valley, in August 1975, are fifteen Folland **Gnat T.1s** of the based No.4 FTS. The station was hosting an air show and had moved many of its aircraft out of the hangars to make room for exhibition displays.

Following basic flying training on the Jet Provost, pilots selected for fast jets would move to RAF Valley for advanced training on the Folland Gnat. Pictured there in August 1975 is **Gnat T.1** XR951 '26' of based No.4 FTS.

Pictured about to land at RAF Valley in September 1971 is **Gnat T.1** XM705 '10' of based No.4 FTS.

Entering RAF service in 1976, the BAe Hawk replaced the Gnat in the advanced training role. It has also been a great export success. Pictured at RAF Valley in August 1977 is **Hawk T.1** XX177 '177' of based No.4 FTS.

As well as its flying training role the RAF uses the Hawk as a weapons trainer. Pictured, in a camouflage scheme, at RAF Leuchars in September 1978 is **Hawk T.1** XX221 '125' of RAF Brawdy-based No.1 TWU (Tactical Weapons Unit).

The Alpha Jet was a joint Dassault and Dornier venture to produce an advanced trainer and light-attack aircraft. It first flew in October 1973. Pictured at Farnborough in September 1978 is Dassault-built **Alpha Jet** E2 118-BQ of CEAM (Centre d'Expérimentations Aériennes Militaires). This unit's role is to evaluate new aircraft types and train pilots for them. This aircraft crashed a week later whilst on a demonstration flight in Egypt.

The market for the advanced jet trainer with ground-attack capability is very competitive; from Eastern Europe the contender was the Czechoslovakian Aero L-39. It entered service in its native country in 1974 and has sold well to over twenty air arms around the world. Pictured at Paris-Le Bourget in June 1977 is **L-39 Albatros** OK-HXA operated by the manufacturer.

The de Havilland Canada Chipmunk first flew in 1946 and was a two-seat elementary trainer. The RAF purchased over 700 and by the start of the decade it was still in service with the University Air Squadrons and Air Experience Flights. Pictured at its RAF Coningsby base in August 1976 is **Chipmunk T.10** WP855 operated by the Battle of Britain Memorial Flight. Its role was to convert fast jet pilots to handling a tail-dragger before they flew the unit's Hurricanes and Spitfires.

An elementary military trainer development of the Beagle Pup, the Bulldog was taken over by Scottish Aviation following the demise of Beagle at the end of the 1960s. The prototype first flew in February 1971 and over 300 aircraft were produced, including 135 for the RAF. It replaced the Chipmunk in the University Air Squadrons and also provided initial pilot training for the RAF and Fleet Air Arm. Pictured at RAF Valley in August 1975 is **Bulldog T.1** XX519 '1' of the RNEFTS (Royal Naval Elementary Flying Training School), a unit embedded into RAF Leeming-based No.3 FTS.

The Scottish Aviation Bulldog sold to four other countries. Pictured at Farnborough in September 1974, prior to delivery, is **Bulldog 123** NAF 238 (G-BBPF) of the Nigerian Air Force.

Switzerland has a long history of building excellent training aircraft. First flown in September 1953, the Pilatus P.3 was a basic trainer with a tricycle undercarriage and powered by a 260hp Lycoming piston engine. Pictured at Locarno in July 1970 is **Pilatus P-3** A-810 of the Swiss Air Force. Its replacement was the PC-7 from the same manufacturer.

The bulk of the production of the Cessna 172 has gone to the civil market for flying clubs and private touring owners. Some military use can be found in various places. One such is the Irish Air Corps where its duties include target-towing, parachuting and army co-operation. Pictured at its Baldonnel/Casement base in August 1977 is Reims-built **Cessna FR.172** 207.

The Italian-built SIAI-Marchetti 260 is a fully aerobatic basic trainer that has a secondary role in armed counter-insurgency operations. Entering service with the Irish Air Corps in 1977 and pictured at its Baldonnel/Casement base in August of that year is **SF-260WE Warrior** 228.

Winner of the competition to build the replacement for the T-6 Texan/Harvard was that aircraft's manufacturer, North American. The new design was the T-28. Following service with the USAF it was adopted by the US Navy but with a more powerful engine, a 1425hp Wright R-1830 Cyclone radial piston. Pictured at NAS Lemoore, California in October 1979 is **T-28B Trojan** 138271 094/NJ of VA-122 *Flying Eagles*. This unit was the based training unit for the A-7 Corsair II and the T-28s would be used as squadron hacks.

A carrier-borne, anti-submarine and early warning aircraft, the Fairey Gannet first flew in 1949 and was powered by a single Armstrong Siddeley Double Mamba turboprop driving contra-props. By the 1970s the only operational role was in airborne early warning. Pictured at its RAF Lossiemouth base in September 1977 is **Gannet T.4** XG888 71/LM of 849 Squadron. This variant was the trainer for the type and 849 was the only Gannet squadron, operating both training and operational aircraft.

Operating a similar role to the Gannet is the French Breguet Alizé. This aircraft is powered by a single Rolls-Royce Dart turboprop. Pictured at Greenham Common in June 1977 is **BR.1050 Alizé** No.51 of Lann-Bihoué-based 4 Flotille of the French Navy.

Designed by North American Rockwell, the OV-10 was a COIN (Counter Insurgency) aircraft. With twin seats, its role was light-attack and forward air control. Pictured at Upper Heyford in July 1976 is **OV-10A Bronco** 68-3799 of the 20th TASS (Tactical Air Support Squadron), part of the 601st TCW based at Sembach, West Germany.

The Grumman Mohawk was first used by the US Army in 1961; its role is surveillance of the battlefield and gathering intelligence. Over the years its systems have been updated. Pictured at Mildenhall in July 1976 is **OV-1D Mohawk** 69-17019 operated by the 73rd Military Intelligence Company of the US Army.

Designed and built in Argentina, the FMA Pucara is a twin-engine turboprop light-attack and close battlefield support aircraft. As well as its guns it has both wing and fuselage hardpoints for weapons carriage. Pictured at Paris-Le Bourget in June 1977 is **IA-58 Pucara** A-507 of the Argentine Air Force.

Developed from the civil Cessna 337 Super Skymaster, the O-2 was a platform for forward air controllers. Under the wings were hardpoints for such stores as target marker rockets and the doors had clear panels for extra visibility. Pictured at Harlingen, Texas in October 1979 is **Cessna O-2A** 69-7667.

The Morane-Saulnier Paris was a four-seat jet-powered liaison aircraft. The powerplants were a pair of Turbomeca Marboré turbojets of 882lb (400kg) static thrust. Pictured at Greenham Common in July 1974 is **MS.760 Paris** No.33 (callsign F-YETD) of the French Navy.

A popular business aircraft, the Aero Commander has served in small numbers in all three major US forces. Its role is that of liaison and staff transport. Pictured at NAS Lemoore, California in October 1979 is **Aero Commander RU-9A** 576184 operated by the US Navy from its China Lake site. It is an ex-US Army machine and had been used by them as a radar test bed for the Mohawk. Note that when the US Navy uses ex USAF and Army aircraft they run the full serial without any gaps.

Another business aircraft adapted by the American military for liaison and staff transport was the Beech Twin Bonanza. In US Army service it was known as the Seminole. Pictured at its base at Heidelberg, West Germany in July 1970 is **U-8D Seminole** 56-3718 of the US Army. Its serial presentation on the aircraft is prefixed '0' to designate that the aircraft was over ten years old, at that time considered long service. This prefix has since been dropped as the current long lifespan of military aircraft has made it unworkable.

A STOL light transport aircraft with the ability to land on unprepared strips, the de Havilland Canada Beaver first flew in 1947. The US military purchased nearly 1000 aircraft, split between the Air Force and the Army. Pictured in July 1970 at its base in Heidelberg, West Germany is **U-6A Beaver** 56-0387 of the US Army. Still in full colour markings with gloss green paint overall, the aircraft has the '0' prefix on the serial presentation denoting that it is over ten years old.

Operating just nine Beavers, the Royal Netherlands Air Force obtained the first in November 1956. They were used for army co-operation work. Pictured at Deelen in June 1973 is **DHC-2 (U-6A) Beaver** S-8. It has the badge of 316 Squadron on the fin. This was a Gilze-Rijen-based Northrop NF-5A/B unit, indicating the aircraft's role as a squadron hack.

The Max Holste Broussard was a French equivalent of the Beaver. It had the same engine, a single 450hp Pratt & Whitney R-985 Wasp, similar performance and dimensions. Pictured whilst in store at Châteaudun in June 1977 is **MH.1521M Broussard** No.18 of the French Air Force.

The North American T-6 Texan/Harvard became one of the world's most widely used advanced trainers. During the 1970s three could be found in service with the A&AEE at Boscombe Down, their role being low-speed chase aircraft for trials and photography. Pictured at Greenham Common in July 1974 is **Harvard T.2B** KF314.

Lockheed's U-2 was developed in great secrecy during the 1950s with the sole aim of overflying the Soviet Union on photographic reconnaissance missions. The airframe has been developed, along with the engine, over the years and it remains in service to this day. Pictured at Edwards AFB in October 1979 is **Lockheed U-2A** 56-6722. This aircraft had been used over the years to test various equipment. Note the skunk on the fin, a reference to the Lockheed plant they were designed in.

One of the first purpose-built business jets, the de Havilland 125 joined the RAF in 1966; its role was as a navigator trainer. Pictured at RAF Valley in August 1973 is **Dominie T.1** XS712 'A' of RAF Finningley-based No.6 FTS. It is in the standard red and white training colours of the period.

As well as the training role of the 125 a later batch was acquired as VIP transport aircraft flying government ministers and senior military staff. Pictured landing at RAF Leuchars in September 1974 is **Dominie CC.2** XX508 of RAF Northolt-based 32 Squadron.

Originally designed by Handley Page, the production of the Jetstream was taken over by Scottish Aviation (later part of BAe) at their Prestwick plant following the demise of Handley Page. Its role in the RAF has been advanced training for pilots who were going on to fly multi-engined types after finishing their Jet Provost course. Pictured at RAF Leuchars in September 1974 is **Jetstream T.1** XX481 '81' of RAF Oakington-based No.5 FTS.

Purchased 'off the shelf' by the US military the North American Sabreliner was used in a number of roles including VIP transport. Pictured at RAF Leuchars in September 1976 is **VT-39 Sabreliner** 61-0685.

The Gulfstream series of business jets can be found in many air arms around the world. Their roles are varied but most are VIP transports, often being the head of state's personal transport. The US Coast Guard operated a single Gulfstream for VIP operations from its base at Washington-National Airport. Pictured at Paris-Le Bourget in June 1977 is **VC-11A Gulfstream II** 01.

The USAF requirement for a utility transport had two competing designs, the McDonnell 119 and the winner, the Lockheed JetStar. It first flew in September 1957 as a twin-engined aircraft but production airframes had four rear-mounted engines. Pictured at Greenham Common in June 1979 is **VC-140B JetStar** 62-4198 of the 58th MAS based at Ramstein, West Germany.

Designed as an Anson replacement for the RAF, the Percival Pembroke was a development from the Prince. It also had a secondary role as a photo reconnaissance platform with six aircraft being built for this task. Pictured at its RAF Wildenrath base in June 1978 is **Pembroke C.1** XL953 of 60 Squadron.

The de Havilland Dove was a twin-engine feeder-liner and business aircraft. It first flew in September 1945 and sold in both the civil and military markets worldwide. Pictured at RAF Leuchars in September 1976 is **Devon C.2/2** WB530 of RAF Northolt-based 207 Sqn. The Devon was the RAF name for the type.

The Scottish Aviation Twin Pioneer was a STOL light transport of very rugged construction. It was simple to maintain, having a fixed undercarriage. Power came from a pair of 640hp Alvis Leonides radial pistons. Most of its RAF career was served 'East of Suez'. The last unit to fly it was the Boscombe Down-based ETPS. This type would be one that few RAF jet or transport pilots had any experience flying and so provided a perfect machine on which to learn the skills of a test pilot. Pictured at Greenham Common in July 1973 is **Twin Pioneer CC.2** XT610 of the ETPS.

Pictured at its Baldonnel/Casement base in August 1977 is Irish Air Corps **de Havilland Dove 8A** 201.

Based upon the Miles Aerovan, the Short SC.7 Skyvan was a light freighter with an uncomplicated design. It first flew in January 1963, and its box-square fuselage and rear loading ramp made it ideal for bulky items. Other uses included parachute training. Pictured at Farnborough in September 1974, prior to delivery, is **Skyvan 3M-400** G450 (G-BCFI) of the air force of Ghana.

When the Avro Anson retired from military service it had led a service life of over thirty years, at that time a very long period. Latterly, its role was as a communications aircraft, with most RAF stations operating one as the Station Flight hack. The RAE at Llanbedr can claim to have operated the last British military Anson. Pictured at Boscombe Down in March 1971 is **Anson C.19** VM352. It has the Welsh Dragon on the nose from its home base.

To replace the Flamant in its liaison and communications role the French Navy purchased twelve Piper Navajos. Pictured at Toussus-le-Noble in May 1977 is **PA-31 Navajo** No.916 of 3S (Escadrille de Servitude) based at Hyeres.

A simple light transport, freighter and communications aircraft, the Dornier Skyservant was built at Oberpfaffenhofen for both the Luftwaffe and Bundesmarine. Over one hundred aircraft were constructed. Pictured at Paris-Le Bourget in June 1977 is **Do.28D-2 Skyservant** 58+97. It served Luftwaffe RF-4E unit AKG 51 at Bremgarten as its communications aircraft.

Powered by a pair of Rolls-Royce Tyne turboprops, the Transall was a joint project between the French and West Germans for a medium size transport aircraft. Pictured at Mildenhall in July 1976 is **Transall C-160D** 50+81 operated by LTG-63 (Air Transport Wing) based at Ahlhorn.

In the mid 1950s there was a quest amongst manufacturers to design and produce the 'DC-3 Replacement'. By far the most successful, in terms of sales, was the Dutch Fokker company with the Friendship. It was first flown in November 1955 and was powered by a pair of Rolls-Royce Dart turboprops. Pictured at Deelen in June 1973 is **F.27 Friendship C-2** of Soesterberg-based 334 Squadron. This was operated as a passenger aircraft by the Royal Netherlands Air Force squadron.

As well as the passenger-equipped Friendship, Fokker developed a military variant with a cargo door and strengthened floor. Pictured at Farnborough in September 1974, prior to delivery, is **F.27-400M Troopship** 5-218 (PH-EXI) of the Imperial Iranian Air Force.

The second of three four-engined airliner designs produced by Douglas was the DC-6. It had a long career in both civil and military fields. Its role was that of a passenger and cargo carrier. The military variants had cargo doors and strengthened floors. Pictured at Greenham Common in July 1974 is **C-118A Liftmaster** 53-3273 of the 7101st ABW (Air Base Wing) based at Wiesbaden, West Germany.

The Belgian Air Force operated four examples of the DC-6; all were purchased from the civil market. Pictured at Liverpool-Speke in April 1971 is **Douglas DC-6** KY-3 (OT-CDC) operated by 21 Smaldeel based at Brussels-Melsbroek. Its visit was to bring in a Belgian Army band to perform in Southport. (Phil Butler)

It is unlikely that any decade of military aviation for many years to come will not feature a Douglas C-47 in some form or other. Pictured at RAF Abingdon in September 1979 is **Dakota C.3** ZA947 of the Farnborough-based Royal Aircraft Establishment. This aircraft still serves in the RAF and is operated by the Battle of Britain Memorial Flight as a transport, a training aid for Lancaster pilots, and as a display aircraft in its own right.

Developed from the Chase C-20 glider, the Fairchild Provider was a twin-engine transport with rough field performance. To boost its take-off run some variants had a pair of J85 jets of 2850lb static thrust mounted under the wings. Pictured at Harlingen, Texas in October 1979 is **C-123K Provider** 54-0580 operated by the US Air Force Reserve.

The Flying Boxcar was a larger version of the earlier C-82. It was a twin-engine, piston-powered, twin-boom, rear-loading tactical transport. Pictured at North Weald in May 1972 is **Fairchild C-119G** CP-35 (OT-CBO). This Belgian Air Force example is operated by Melsbroek-based 15 Wing.

Used as a transport aircraft until replaced by the C-130, the Handley Page Hastings was a true workhorse of the air. Eight aircraft were converted to instruct bomb aimers in the new world of electronics and radar bombing. Fitted to the underside of the fuselage they had a large radome in which was housed the radar set. It was this batch of aircraft that flew on into the 1970s. Pictured at RAF St Mawgan in July 1974 is **Hastings T.5** TG511 of 230 OCU/SCBS (Strike Command Bombing School) based at RAF Scampton.

The last user of the Valetta, the military version of the Vickers Viking, was the A&AEE at Boscombe Down. The variant was fitted with a cargo door and strengthened floor. This last aircraft, **Valetta C.1** WJ941, is pictured at base in March 1971.

The role of the Vickers Varsity was twofold. One was to provide advanced flying training for pilots bound for multi-engined types and the other was to teach bomb aimers and navigators their craft. The aircraft was equipped with an under-fuselage pannier fitted with a bomb aiming position and rear doors for practice bombs. Pictured at RAF Valley in August 1973 is **Varsity T.1** WF331 'M' of RAF Oakington-based No.5 FTS.

Despite it being one of the most successful civil airliners ever produced in Britain, the Vickers Viscount only had limited military sales. In the UK a small number of aircraft have been used for various tests and trials. Pictured at RAF Abingdon in September 1979 is **Viscount 837** XT575 of the RAE's Bedford base. Note this has a large dome under the front fuselage.

Built in Canada, the Buffalo is part of a long line of STOL go-anywhere transport aircraft from de Havilland Canada. Pictured at Paris-Orly in June 1977 is **DHC-5D Buffalo** 5V-MAG of the Togo Air Force. This small African air force had purchased two the previous year to replace its C-47s.

A twin-engine, high-wing light transport, the Nord 262 was developed from the earlier 260. It has been sold to both civil and military operators. Pictured at Toussus-le-Noble in May 1977 is **Nord 262A** No.51 of the French Navy unit SSD (Section de Soutien de Dugny). Based at Le Bourget, its role was to provide transport for members of the Paris-based Naval HQ.

The Short SC.5 Belfast had just ten years of service life before defence cuts ended its operations in 1976. It was a long-range strategic freighter with a high bulk capacity. Pictured at RAF Leuchars in September 1974 is **Belfast C.1** XR371 of 53 Squadron. This RAF Brize Norton-based unit was the only squadron to operate the type.

Another victim of defence cuts was the Bristol Britannia. A long-range troop carrier powered by four turboprops, it entered service with the RAF in 1959. Pictured at RAF St Mawgan in August 1974 is **Britannia C.1** XM489 of RAF Lyneham-based 99 Squadron. 1976 saw the type retired.

The last military Blackburn Beverley was operated, like so many types, by the A&AEE at Boscombe Down. It was a large box-like freighter that first flew in June 1950 and left regular RAF service in 1967. Pictured at its base in March 1971 is **Beverley C.1** XB261 of the A&AEE.

A French-built transport, the Nord Noratlas had a high wing and twin booms. As well as its native air force it served in Germany, Greece, Israel, Niger and Portugal. Pictured at Lakenheath in August 1975 is **N.2501 Noratlas** No.63 312-BH of 312 Groupement Instruction. It is the support aircraft for the *Patrouille de France* aerobatic team and has the unit's badge on the nose.

As well as transport roles the large capacity of the Noratlas made it useful for test work. Pictured at Châteaudun in June 1977 is **N.2501 Noratlas** No.29 of the Bretigny-based CEV (Centre d'Essais en Vol), a research institute. It is of note that this aircraft has non-standard wing tips.

The Convair range of twin-engined airliners found large sales with the US Military. The original production CV-240 was purchased as a navigation trainer and then as a transport. Pictured at Bentwaters in May 1972 is **Convair T-29B** 51-7892 of the Mildenhall-based 513th TAW (Tactical Airlift Wing).

Based upon the CV-340, the US Navy operated the popular twin for many years as a general transport aircraft. Pictured in August 1978 at its Mildenhall base is **Convair C-131F** 141023 operated by the Station Flight.

A development from the Avro (Hawker Siddeley) 748 airliner, the Andover was designed for the military user. As well as having a rear cargo door that could open in flight to air drop supplies, the undercarriage was able to 'kneel' to bring the loading ramp down to ground level. Pictured at RAF Leuchars in September 1974 is **Andover C.1** XS612 of 46 Squadron.

Powered by four Rolls-Royce Dart turboprops, the Armstrong Whitworth Argosy was a twin-boom, medium-range tactical freighter. It entered service with the RAF in 1962; following its withdrawal as a transport a small number of aircraft were converted to the role of electronic calibrators. Pictured at RAF Abingdon in June 1977 is **Argosy E.1** XN855 of RAF Brize Norton-based 115 Squadron.

When the A&AEE operate an aircraft it will usually be in different livery to normal squadron ones. Such a case is pictured here, **Argosy C.1** XN817, seen at RAF Coltishall in September 1971.

By the 1970s the military variant of the Stratocruiser, the C-97, was mainly to be found in the flying tanker role operated by Air National Guard units in the USA. Pictured at Greenham Common in July 1974 is **Boeing KC-97L** 52-2630 operated by the 145th ARS (Air Refuelling Squadron) Ohio ANG based at Rickenbacker AFB.

As well as its four Pratt & Whitney R-4360 radial pistons of 3500hp each the 'L' model of the KC-97 had a single J47 jet under each wing to boost power. Seen flying over Greenham Common in July 1974, with all six engines turning or burning, is **Boeing KC-97L** 52-2630 operated by the 145th ARS Ohio ANG.

That most elegant of airliners, the Lockheed Constellation had a long and varied military career. Pictured at Greenham Common in July 1974 is **Lockheed C-121C** 54-0157 operated by the 193rd TEWS (Tactical Electronic Warfare Squadron) of the Pennsylvania ANG based at Harrisburg. This aircraft is now flying in Australia with the Historic Aircraft Restoration Society.

First championed by the US Navy, the early 1950s saw the birth of what we would today call AWACS. Radar sets were fitted both above and below the fuselages of Constellations. The USAF followed and operated their own variants. Pictured at Mildenhall in August 1978 is **Lockheed EC-121T** 54-2307 operated by the 20th ADS (Air Defence Squadron) Det.1 based at Keflavik, Iceland.

Pictured at its Homestead AFB base, Florida in July 1974 is **Lockheed EC-121T** 52-3417 of the 79th AEW&C (Airborne Early Warning & Control) Squadron of the AFRES (Air Force Reserve). (Phil Butler)

US Navy **Lockheed EC-121K** 145939 10/GD of VAQ-33 *Firebirds* is pictured at its NAS Norfolk, Virginia base in May 1972. The unit's role was to provide electronic warfare training to the ships of the fleet; as well as the EC-121 it also operated a variety of jets. (Phil Butler)

The current transport workhorse of the world's air forces is the Lockheed Hercules. It first flew in 1952 and has had an unbroken production run since that date, a record for any aircraft type. Pictured at RAF Leuchars in September 1977 is **C-130K Hercules C.1** XV199 based at RAF Lyneham. The transport wing at that base has central servicing so the fleet do not usually carry individual squadron markings.

One of the oddest Hercules flying was the aircraft operated by the RAE for meteorological research. The nose radar has been repositioned onto the cockpit roof to accommodate an 18ft (5.49m)-long instrumentation boom. **Hercules W.2** XV208 is pictured at RAF Leuchars in September 1975.

As to be expected the US military is the largest user of the C-130. Pictured at Lakenheath in August 1975 is **C-130E Hercules** 70-1274 operated by the 39th TAS/317th TAW Military Airlift Command. Despite its camouflage it still has gloss paint and full colour unit and national markings.

Pictured at its Heywood base in October 1979 is **HC-130P Hercules** 66-0224 operated by the 129th Rescue Squadron, California ANG. Its role was the combat rescue of aircrew.

The US Coast Guard has always had one of the smartest colour schemes applied to any aircraft. Pictured departing Greenham Common in June 1979 is **HC-130H Hercules** 1602 based at Kodiak, Alaska.

The use of the BAC One-Eleven airliner has, in the UK, been limited to test work for various trials with the RAE. Pictured at Greenham Common in June 1979 is **BAC One-Eleven 402AP** XX919, part of the Farnborough-based RAE fleet.

Boeing's 737 is the best selling jet airliner in the world. It has however had only limited military sales. The USAF operates them as navigation training aircraft. Pictured at Travis AFB, California in October 1979 is **Boeing T-43A** 73-1151 of the Mather AFB-based 323rd FTW.

The purchase of the Douglas DC-9 airliner by the USAF gave them an airframe to customise in the role of aeromedical evacuation. All the fleet carry a red cross on the fin. Pictured at Greenham Common in July 1973 is **C-9A Nightingale** 71-0881 of the 322nd TAW.

During the 1970s the sole use of the Vickers VC-10 in RAF service was in the passenger transport role, taking troops to their bases worldwide. Pictured flying at RAF Coltishall in September 1971 is **VC-10 C.1** XV101 of RAF Brize Norton-based 10 Squadron.

Entering service with the USAF in 1964, the Lockheed Starlifter was a huge leap in performance over such types as the C-124. Pictured at Mildenhall in May 1977 is **C-141A Starlifter** 65-0218 of the 437th MAW Military Airlift Command.

The largest cargo carrier with the USAF is the Lockheed Galaxy. It has the capacity for 265,000lb of cargo or 350 troops. It can be loaded either through the nose or via the tail ramp. Pictured at Greenham Common in June 1979 is **C-5A Galaxy** 68-0217 of the 436th MAW Military Airlift Command based at Dover AFB, Delaware. It is in the original white and grey colours that the fleet first operated in prior to the current camouflage.

The military uses of the Boeing 707 family have only been limited by the imagination of engineers. The largest use has been with the USAF as flying tankers, with over 700 being procured. Pictured at its Castle AFB base, California in October 1979 is **Boeing KC-135A** 60-0320 of the 93rd BW (Bomb Wing). Tanking was regarded as so important to SAC (Strategic Air Command) that each wing of bombers had its own dedicated tankers based with it.

To power the engines of the Lockheed SR-71 a special fuel, called JP-7, had to be devised to cope with the extreme altitude and speed that it flew at. The normal KC-135s themselves used and dispensed to other aircraft JP-4. To feed the SR-71 fleet fifty-six KC-135s were converted to 'Q' standard to dispense JP-7 and had their own JP-4 isolated so as to just feed their own engines. Pictured landing at Mildenhall in August 1976 is **Boeing KC-135Q** 58-0089 of the 17th BW.

The EC-135 variant is a flying command post with a senior officer on board and a vast range of communications systems to cope with critical situations. Pictured landing at Mildenhall in August 1976 is **Boeing EC-135H** 61-0282 of the 10th ACCS (Airborne Control & Communications Squadron).

A revolving 30ft (9.14m)-diameter rotodome to house its radar sets the AWACS (Airborne Warning and Control System) variant of the 707 apart. The system has since been sold to the RAF, NATO and Saudi Air Force. Pictured at Paris-Le Bourget in June 1977 is **Boeing E-3A Sentry** 73-1675 operated by the Tinker AFB, Oklahoma-based 552nd AW&CW and currently on loan to Boeing for trials.

Before the 1979 revolution the Imperial Iranian Air Force spent vast amounts of money on American equipment. It was for both front-line and support aircraft. Pictured at Farnborough in September 1976, prior to delivery, is **Boeing 707-3J9C** 5-249 a new-build tanker. This has the hose and drogue system fitted as well as the flying boom used by the USAF.

One of the most widely used maritime patrol aircraft, with a long service life, was the Lockheed Neptune. Pictured at RAF St Mawgan in August 1974 is **SP-2H Neptune** 202 operated by 320 Squadron of the Royal Netherlands Navy based at Valkenburg. This variant was the last main production version and features a single Westinghouse J34 turbojet of 3400lb static thrust under each wing. The non-standard white upper surface of the fuselage was for service with the squadron detachment at Hato in the Dutch West Indies.

The French Navy was another user of the Neptune. Pictured at Greenham Common in July 1973 is **SP-2H Neptune** (147)562 of 25 Flotille based at Lann-Blhoué. The aircraft were supplied to France under the Military Aid Program and had US Navy serials, the French using just the last three numbers of these.

The sole user of the Canadair Argus was its manufacturing nation, Canada. It was a maritime patrol aircraft based upon the Bristol Britannia, but only the wings, tail surfaces and undercarriage remained the same. Pressurisation and turboprops were not deemed to be needed for very long low-level overwater flights. It first flew in March 1957 and entered service the same year. Pictured at RAF St Mawgan in August 1974 is **CP-107 Argus 2** 10741 of 449 *Unicorn* Squadron CAF. This unit was based at Greenwood, Nova Scotia and was the training squadron for the type.

The last and largest of a line of Grumman amphibians, the Albatross first flew in 1947 and was sold worldwide to air arms as both a rescue and a patrol aircraft. Pictured at their Palma-Majorca base in November 1973 is **HU-16B Albatross** AD.1B-10 of Escuadron 801, a search and rescue unit of the Spanish Air Force.

Powered by a pair of Rolls-Royce Tyne turboprops, the Breguet Atlantic first flew in 1961. Its role was as a maritime patrol aircraft and it has operated with five air arms. Pictured at Lakenheath in August 1975 is **BR.1150 Atlantic** 61+16 of West German Navy unit MFG3. They were based at Nordholz.

Pictured at RAF St Mawgan in August 1974 is **BR.1150 Atlantic** 254 of Valkenburg-based 321 Squadron of the Royal Netherlands Navy. They received nine aircraft, the first in 1969, but only operated them for a few years before replacing them with the P-3 Orion.

The most widely used Western-built maritime patrol aircraft is the Lockheed Orion. This four-engined turboprop is a direct development of the L-188 Electra airliner, but with a shorter fuselage. Pictured at Edwards AFB in October 1979 is **P-3A Orion** 152166 3/PG of US Navy Patrol Squadron VP-65 *Tridents*. This reserve unit is based at NAS Point Mugu, California.

Pictured at Lakenheath in August 1975 is **P-3C Orion** 158921 'LF' of NAS Jacksonville, Florida-based VP-16 *Eagles*. This was a time when all the markings were in full gloss colours. Today P-3s fly in a matt grey with grey markings and usually without any squadron identity.

To patrol its vast coastlines Canada chose the P-3 to replace the Argus and bases its fleet on either coast. Pictured at NAS Point Mugu in October 1979 is **CP-140 Aurora** 140101/N64996. This first CAF aircraft had not yet been delivered from Lockheed so still carried a civil registration.

Despite its age and its replacement by the Nimrod in the maritime patrol role, the Avro Shackleton found a new lease of life in the decade as an AEW (Airborne Early Warning) aircraft. It carried the radar set under the nose. Pictured at RAF Leuchars in September 1974 is **Shackleton AEW.2** WR960 of RAF Lossiemouth-based 8 Squadron. It is of note that the Shackleton airframes used were the tailwheel-equipped MR.2s rather than the more modern tricycle undercarriage MR.3s

Pictured flying at RAF Leuchars in September 1975 is **Shackleton AEW.2** WR965 of 8 Squadron. This RAF Lossiemouth-based unit was the sole user of the type in this role.

Keeping up the tradition of operating 'the last in service' of a type is tricycle undercarriage **Shackleton MR.3** WR972 of the Royal Aircraft Establishment. It is seen at its Boscombe Down base in March 1971, in a non-standard livery for the type.

The replacement for the Shackleton in the maritime role was the Hawker Siddeley Nimrod. This was a direct development from the Comet airliner. Pictured at Boscombe Down in March 1971 is the first prototype **HS.801 Nimrod** XV148. This aircraft was built at Chester from one of the last Comet 4C airframes and first flew in May 1967. It was powered by four Rolls-Royce Spey turbofans. This aircraft is undergoing weapons trials with an under-wing missile fitted.

Pictured landing at Farnborough in September 1976 is **Nimrod MR.1** XZ282. This aircraft is from the RAF Kinloss Wing; because they are centrally serviced individual aircraft do not carry squadron markings.

One of the most versatile and long-serving aircraft has been the English Electric Canberra. It first flew in 1948 and only left RAF service in 2006. Pictured at its Boscombe Down base in March 1971 is **Canberra B.2(Mod)** WH734. This A&AEE aircraft has been converted to a flying tanker for air-to-air refuelling trials.

Pictured at its RAF Cottesmore base in May 1972 is **Canberra T.4** WT480 'B' of 231 OCU. This variant was the trainer for the type and the unit was the conversion unit for new pilots.

The Canberra T.17 was used for electronic counter-measures training and had a re-shaped nose. Pictured at RAF Leuchars in September 1975 is **Canberra T.17** WJ981 'S' of 360 Squadron. This was a unique unit within the RAF as it had been formed in October 1966 for the first time and had not had a wartime history. It was a joint RAF/RN unit based at RAF Wyton.

Pictured at RAF Leuchars in September 1974 is **Canberra T.19** WJ975 'X' of 100 Squadron. This aircraft had been built as a B.2 and then converted to the big-nose T.11. This variant was used to train airborne interceptor radar operators. It was lastly converted to a T.19 by having the radar removed as the role of the squadron was to provide flying targets not to track them.

The Canberra was such a good aeroplane that the Americans bought it. They were licence-built by the Glen L. Martin Company in Baltimore. Pictured at RAF Binbrook in August 1978 is **EB-57E Canberra** 55-4263 of the 17th DSES (Defence Systems Evaluation Squadron). It was one of five visiting European bases on an exercise.

First flown in December 1974 the Rockwell B-1A was designed to replace the B-52 with SAC. In 1977 the US President, Jimmy Carter, cancelled the programme but allowed the prototypes to continue testing and trials. Pictured at Edwards AFB in October 1979 is **Rockwell B-1A** 74-0159 operated by the based Air Force Flight Test Centre. The change of president, with Ronald Reagan moving into the White House in 1981, put the programme back into production with a downgraded, for cost purposes, variant known as the B-1B.

The General Dynamics F-111 had one of the most controversial starts in life, in both its development and its first disastrous operational tour. It has, however, matured into a well-proven system with a good combat record. Pictured at Travis AFB, California in October 1979 is **F-111A** 67-0101 of the 366th TFW based at Mountain Home in Idaho.

Following the 'A' model F-111 was the 'E'. It was externally similar but with updates to many systems. Pictured at its Upper Heyford base in July 1976 is **F-111E** 68-0049 operated by the 79th TFS/20th TFW.

The fitting of a much more powerful TF-30 engine resulted in the 'F' model of the F-111. Pictured at its Lakenheath base in May 1979 is **F-111F** 70-2373 of the 495th TFS/ 48th TFW.

The 1976 bi-centennial of the USA was celebrated by the USAF with special markings on many of its aircraft. Pictured in July of that year at Upper Heyford is **F-111E** 68-0028 of the based 20th TFW.

SAC operated its own variant of the F-111. This had longer-span wings, extra fuel and revised avionics for its role as a long-range nuclear bomber. Pictured at George AFB, California in October 1979 is **FB-111A** 68-0281 of the 380th Bomb Wing based at Plattsburg AFB, New York.

What was to become the backbone of the RAF in the future, the Panavia Tornado/MRCA underwent test flights during the 1970s. The first British-built aircraft made its maiden flight, in November 1974, from Warton. Seen at Farnborough in September 1978 is **Tornado P.03** XX947, the second British aircraft and the first with dual controls.

The Douglas Skywarrior was the largest and heaviest aircraft that flew, in regular service, off the decks of the US Navy's aircraft carriers. It first flew in October 1952 and its early life was as an attack-bomber. Later in its career it acted as a tanker and electronic warfare aircraft. Pictured at NAS Norfolk, Virginia in May 1972 is **EKA-3B Skywarrior** 138922 1/GD of Tactical Electronic Warfare Squadron VAQ-33 *Firebirds*. (Phil Butler)

Pictured at Greenham Common in June 1977 is **EA-3B Skywarrior** 144852 '18' of Fleet Air Reconnaissance Squadron VQ-2 *Batman*, shore-based at Rota, Spain. This variant was a radar and recce aircraft that housed four systems operators in a pressurised fuselage area. This unit was the last to operate the type, retiring them in 1992.

The longevity of the B-52 is quite staggering. It first flew in April 1952 and entered service in 1955. The current plans are for it still to be operational in 2040, eighty-five years from joining the USAF. Its role has always been the same – an eight-engined heavy bomber. Pictured at its Castle AFB base in October 1979 is **B-52G Stratofortress** 58-0220 of the 93rd Bomb Wing. The 'G' model was the first variant to have the reduced-size vertical fin.

Pictured in the circuit of its Castle AFB base in October 1979 is **B-52H Stratofortress** 60-0051 of the 93rd BW. The 'H' variant was the first to have the Pratt & Whitney J57 turbojets replaced with TF-33 turbofans. This reduced the huge smoke trail for which the earlier models were renowned.

B-52H Stratofortress 60-0048 of the 93rd BW is pictured under maintenance at its Castle AFB base in October 1979.

Pictured on what was then still a rare UK deployment, to take part in the RAF's Bombing and Navigation Competition at RAF Marham in April 1970, is **B-52H Stratofortress** 60-0037 (presented as 0-00037 as ten-year-old aircraft were still marked) of the 524th BS/379th BW based at Wurtsmith AFB, Michigan.

The Avro Vulcan was the second of the three V-bombers into service. Its original role was delivery of a nuclear bomb but it could also carry conventional weapons. It was distinctive for its delta-wing planform and its fighter-like performance at air shows. By the 1970s all units were equipped with the B.2 variant. Showing off its wing shape at RAF Leuchars in September 1975 is **Vulcan B.2** XM650 of RAF Waddington-based 44 Squadron. The unit equipped with the original B.1 in August 1960, moving to the B.2 by 1967 and eventually disbanded at the end of 1982.

During the 'Cold War' the Vulcan was part of the UK's nuclear deterrent force. With only a 'four minute warning' they spent times of high global tension on cockpit alert with the aircraft parked on specially constructed pans giving instant access to the runway. The four alert aircraft were able to scramble in as little as ninety seconds for the last one to have its wheels off the ground. Pictured at RAF Finningley in July 1977, on the alert pad, is **Vulcan B.2** XL389 of RAF Waddington-based 9 Squadron. The unit had been formed with the type in 1962 and disbanded twenty years later.

Vulcans took on the role of reconnaissance when 543 Squadron was disbanded and its Victor SR.2s converted to tankers. This variant used the Vulcan's existing radar with specific enhancements for the role with regard to navigation equipment. It could also carry atmospheric-sampling pods under the wings. For the new role some items were deleted, these included the terrain-following radar. Pictured at RAF Leuchars in September 1975 is **Vulcan B.2 (MRR)** (Maritime Reconnaissance Role) XH563 of RAF Scampton-based 27 Squadron. This unit had originally converted to the type in 1961, disbanded in March 1972 and reformed with the B.2 (MRR) in November 1973 and continued, as the only unit with the variant, until March 1982. Note this aircraft is fitted with under-wing pods.

The last of the V-bombers to fly in the original white anti-flash scheme was the A&AEE's **Vulcan B.2** XH539. It is pictured, on a wet day, at its Boscombe Down base in March 1971.

The Bell UH-1 Iroquois has been the most widely used helicopter to date. The US Army has operated over 9000 examples since 1958. Its distinctive blade sound was one of the iconic features of the Vietnam War. Pictured at the US Army Europe HQ at Heidelberg, West Germany in July 1970 is **UH-1D Iroquois** 64-13697 operated by the *Flying Mustangs*. It is still in full colour markings with gloss green paint, these soon gave way to matt green and black markings.

The US Navy used the UH-1 for a number of roles; one such was that of Base Rescue Flight at their air stations. Pictured in October 1979 is **UH-1N Iroquois** 158762 as it hovers over the ramp at its NAS Lemoore, California base.

Pictured aboard USS *Guadalcanal* (LPH-7) in October 1978 is **UH-1N Iroquois** 160827 operated as the ship's base flight.

The Iroquois was licence-built in Italy as the Agusta-Bell 204 and entered service in 1963. Pictured at RNAS Lee-on-Solent in July 1972 is **AB-204B** MM80331 15-26 of 15 Stormo, an SAR unit with a Rome-Ciampino HQ.

A ship-borne anti-submarine helicopter, the Kaman Seasprite first flew in 1959. Pictured in August 1970 on board USS *Guadalcanal* (LPH-7) is **VH-2A Seasprite** 149032 157/HT of HC-4 *Black Stallions*.

Designed by Aérospatiale and licence-built in the UK by Westland, the Gazelle can be found in the uniform of all three services. Pictured in July 1972 at RNAS Yeovilton is **Gazelle HT.2** XW845. This was the first of the type for the Fleet Air Arm; its role in service was that of a pilot trainer.

Pictured at RAF Abingdon in September 1979 is **Gazelle HT.3** ZA801 'V' of the Central Flying School. The helicopter section of the CFS is based at RAF Shawbury and its task is to teach flying instructors their art.

The Kaman Huskie first flew in 1958; it was powered by a single 860shp Lycoming T.53 turboshaft driving two intermeshing rotors. It was used by the USAF as a base crash-rescue aircraft and airborne fire-fighter. **HH-43F Huskie** 59-1564 is pictured at RNAS Lee-on-Solent in July 1972.

The Boeing-Vertol Chinook was first flown in 1961 and is a heavy-lift, twin rotor helicopter. Pictured at Paris-Le Bourget in June 1977 is licence-built Agusta Meridionali Boeing **CH-47C Chinook** MM80844 EI-822 of 12 Gruppi Squadroni of the Italian Army (Esercito).

Pictured at Paris-Le Bourget in June 1977 is **Agusta-Bell AB-214ASW** MM80943 7-11 of Italian Navy Gruppo 4. Used for anti-submarine warfare, it has a dome-shaped radar bulge on the cabin roof. Once it has detected a submarine it can attack it with missiles and torpedoes. It is a licence-built Bell 212.

The Bell Jet Ranger is one of the most popular helicopters in both the civil and military market places. Pictured at Paris-Le Bourget in June 1977 is Italian Army licence-built **Agusta-Bell AB-206B** MM80890 EI-622 of 28 Gruppi Squadroni.

The Westland company developed two helicopters in parallel. The Scout, for the Army, was on skids; while the Wasp for the Navy had wheels. Both were basically the same but the roles served were quite different. Pictured at RAF Wildenrath in June 1978 is **Scout AH.1** XP897 of 651 Squadron Army Air Corps based at Verden, West Germany. The AAC used the Scout as a general-purpose machine with the capability to be equipped with anti-tank rockets.

Pictured at RAF Leuchars in September 1976 is **Scout AH.1** XT629 'X' of 3 CBAS (Commando Brigade Air Squadron) Royal Marines.

The Westland Wasp's service in the Royal Navy was to operate off the decks of frigates in the anti-submarine role; it was armed with homing torpedoes and depth charges. Pictured at RNAS Portland in August 1974 is **Wasp HAS.1** XV631 '617' of 829 Squadron HQ Flight. This station was its home base.

Used by the French Navy for ship-borne logistical support, the Aérospatiale Super Frelon is one of the largest helicopters ever built in Europe. Pictured at RNAS Portland in August 1974 is **SA.3210 Super Frelon** No.162 of 32 Flotille based at Lanveoc-Poulmic.

An assault troop-carrier, the Boeing-Vertol Sea Knight first flew in April 1958 and entered service with the US Marine Corps in June 1964. Pictured on the deck of USS *Guadalcanal* (LPH-7) in October 1978 is **CH-46F Sea Knight** 155313 1/YS of HMM-162, shore-based at New River, North Carolina.

Pictured at NAS Point Mugu, California in October 1979 is **HH-46D Sea Knight** 151939 '14' of the base Rescue Flight. This variant was the dedicated SAR version of the type.

The Puma helicopter is a medium-size transport designed by Eurocopter (Aérospatiale) and has been sold widely around the world. In the UK Westland have licence-built the type for service with the RAF. Pictured at RAF Valley in August 1975 is **Puma HC.1** XW221 'DE' of RAF Odiham-based 230 Squadron.

First flying in December 1945, the Bell 47 had developed through a number of models during its lifespan up to the end of production in 1973. The US Army operated over 2000 aircraft, by far the largest user. Pictured at its Heidelberg, West Germany base in July 1970 is **OH-13H Sioux** 56-2166 of the US Army. Some of the roles it fulfilled were casualty evacuation and observation.

The Bell 47 can claim to be one of the first practical and reliable helicopters. It has had extensive service in both civil and military operations. The type was licence-built in the UK by Westland from the Agusta company who had received the original manufacturing licence from Bell. Pictured at RAF Valley in August 1973 is **Sioux HT.2** XV313 'E' of the CFS. The main user of the type in the UK was the Army Air Corps, but a number of machines served the RAF.

When the USAF wants to purchase an existing type of aircraft they often want so many changes that it begins to look quite different. The H-3 was based upon the SH-3 Sea King but changes included a new undercarriage and a rear loading door. Pictured at Luke AFB, Arizona in October 1979 is **Sikorsky CH-3E** 65-5697 operated by the based 302nd SOS (Special Operations Squadron) Air Force Reserve.

To replace the H-3 in the SAR role the USAF looked at the H-53, operated by the USMC as a heavy-lift transport, and adapted it for the new task. Pictured at Lakenheath in August 1975 is **Sikorsky HH-53C** 73-1647 of the 67th ARRS (Aerospace Rescue & Recovery Squadron).

Operated by the Royal Navy as a basic training helicopter, the Hiller HT.2 was in service until 1975. Pictured at RNAS Portland in August 1974 is **Hiller HT.2** XS162 '48' of 705 Squadron based at RNAS Culdrose.

Another type operated by both the Army and Royal Navy is the Westland Lynx. This original design has sold well to air arms around the world. Its roles are to replace those of the Scout and Wasp. Pictured at RAF Abingdon in September 1979 is **Lynx HAS.2** XZ251 '746' of RNAS Yeovilton-based 702 Squadron. This aircraft was destroyed in May 1982, whilst serving on board HMS *Ardent* in the Falklands conflict.

The Sikorsky S-55 was licence-built by Westland as the Whirlwind. Originally powered by an Alvis piston engine, later versions were built with a Bristol Siddeley Gnome 1050shp turboprop. Pictured at RAF Finningley in July 1977 is **Whirlwind HAR.10** XP403 of 202 Squadron. The role of this squadron was search and rescue, hence the well known yellow scheme. The unit's aircraft were split between four bases along the east coast.

Pictured at RAF Finningley in July 1977 is **Whirlwind HAR.10** XD163 'X' of RAF Shawbury-based No. 2 FTS, the RAF's helicopter training unit. This airframe had been built with a piston power plant but re-engined with the Gnome turboprop.

The Royal Navy was a major user of the Whirlwind in a number of roles. Pictured flying over RNAS Lee-on-Solent in July 1974 are **Whirlwind HAR.9s** XN298 '10' and XN311 '12' of the based Search and Rescue Flight.

Following the S-55, Sikorsky produced the S-58/H-34 Choctaw; this was sold by the manufacturer or available in licence-built versions. One of the former is pictured at RNAS Lee-on-Solent in July 1972; it is **SH-34 Choctaw** 80+94 of the West German Navy. It is operated by Kiel-based MFG.5.

The H-34 was built in France under licence by Sud Aviation. As well as French use it was supplied to Belgium. Pictured at RNAS Lee-on-Solent in July 1972 is **Sikorsky-Sud S-58** B5 (OT-ZKE) of 40 Heli-Smaldeel based at Koksijde.

In the UK the S-58 was built by Westland under licence. Early British aircraft had a Napier Gazelle gas turbine engine, as opposed to US and French machines that were all still piston-powered. Later production had two coupled Bristol Siddeley Gnome 1350shp turboshafts. Pictured at its RNAS Portland base in August 1974 is **Wessex HAS.3** XP140 of 737 Squadron, the type's training unit. The role of this variant was anti-submarine and it could be armed with a pair of homing torpedoes.

One of the roles for the Royal Navy was the transporting of commandoes of the Royal Marines into action. A version of the Wessex was developed for this and, as well as its transport capacity, it could be fitted with guns or wire-guided missiles. Pictured flying at RNAS Lee-on-Solent in July 1974 is **Wessex HU.5** XS508 'V-M' of 848 Squadron. This unit was carrier-based aboard HMS *Bulwark*.

The transport of the British Army has been the role of the RAF and they too operated the Wessex in this task. As with the navy variants the airframe had to be strengthened to overcome the rigours of constant low-level operations. Pictured flying at Farnborough in September 1976 is **Wessex HC.2** XR517 'AN' of RAF Odiham-based 72 Squadron.

The Wessex replaced the Whirlwind in the RAF's Search and Rescue squadrons and adopted the well-known yellow livery. Pictured flying at RAF Leuchars in September 1977 is **Wessex HAR.2** XR497 of 22 Squadron. As with the Whirlwind, the unit's aircraft were based at several detachments around the coast of the UK.

Sikorsky's Sea King has been one of the most widely used helicopters, especially for maritime operations. Pictured at RNAS Lee-on-Solent in July 1972 is **S-61A Sea King** U-280 of Esk 722 of the Danish Air Force. The unit was based at Vaerlose for SAR work but had detachments at several other bases.

Licence production of the Sea King in the UK was in the capable hands of Westland. They have kept the design up to date and have now out-sold the US production. One of their sales was to Australia. Pictured at Greenham Common in June 1977 is **Sea King Mk.50** N16-125 '10' of Royal Australian Navy squadron HS017. The unit's role was anti-submarine, operating from the carrier HMAS *Melbourne*. When this ship was retired they redeployed on to support ships and have taken on such roles as SAR and supply. They are shore-based at Nowra.

The Fleet Air Arm have used the Sea King for many roles, these include SAR, troop transports, anti-submarine and in more recent years AEW. Pictured at RAF Valley in August 1973 is **Sea King HAS.1** XV713 412/BL of 820 Squadron. This is an anti-submarine unit ship-based on HMS *Blake* and shore-based at RNAS Culdrose.

The sale to over twenty-five countries of the Alouette II gives testimony to how successful a general-purpose light helicopter Sud Aviation (now Aérospatiale) built. Pictured at Paris-Issy in May 1977 is **Alouette II** No.1282 67-SD of French Air Force squadron EH 3/67 *Parisis*. This unit was based at Villacoublay.

The Alouette III was developed from the earlier model. Its most obvious feature was the larger cabin. As well as this it had a more powerful engine and other assorted equipment upgrades. This too has sold well around the world. Pictured at RNAS Lee-on-Solent in July 1972 is **Alouette III** M-019 of the Danish Naval Air Service. It was based at Vaerlose and the aircraft was maintained by the air force unit Esk 722. Note that it has large inflatable floats.

Pictured at its Baldonnel/Casement base in August 1977 is **SE.3160 Alouette III** 212 of the Irish Air Corps. A total of eight served the air arm and its duties included SAR as well as army liaison and support.

The role of the Sikorsky S-64 Skycrane was as a heavy-lift flying crane for the US Army. As well as its lift capacity it could also carry a special cargo pod that the very tall undercarriage would straddle. Pictured at North Weald in May 1972 is **CH-54A Tarhe** 67-18448 of the 295th Aviation Company.

In the early 1960s the US Army saw the need for a specialist armed attack helicopter. The war in Vietnam accelerated this and, following a fly-off competition, the winner was the Bell AH-1. This was first flown in September 1965 and took part in the fly-off the following spring. Service entry with the US Army began in May 1967. Pictured at Greenham Common in July 1973 is **AH-1G Huey Cobra** 70-16003 of the 60th Aviation Company. The design has been continually updated and it has sold to more than ten air arms.

Index of Types